Straight Talk for
Smart Business Women

Straight Talk for *Smart* Business Women

Critical Tools to Build & Grow Your Business

Cheryl Leitschuh, Ed.D.

Cover design by: Clark Kenyon
Stock image via: iStock
CALM© graphics designed by: Jennifer Wreisner, One18 Design

Printed in the United States of America

ISBN-13: 978-1983949418
ISBN-10: 1983949418

Author's Website: www.CherylLeitschuh.com

About the Author

Mentor, guide, and influencer, many of Cheryl's clients describe her as the "Yoda" for solopreneurs and woman-owned small businesses.

Cheryl has had the pleasure of owning a successful, sustainable small business for over twenty-five years. She has stumbled, regrouped, learned, succeeded, and failed, BUT has remained committed to being an entrepreneur. Cheryl has also coached other woman-owned small businesses to capitalize on their opportunities. Her mission is to help woman-owned small businesses to start, build, and grow their own successful enterprise.

Cheryl has created a nationally- and internationally-known business as a consultant, coach, author, and speaker with a focus on leadership development. She has authored five books, created *The Leadership Energy Model*, and won awards for innovation as part of her entrepreneurial business.

Cheryl is listed in *Who's Who of American Women* and *Who's Who of Professional Women*. She is a past Chair of the AICPA Women's Initiative and Work/Life Balance Committee. She has served as a board member of Wayside House (a chemical dependency treatment program for women), participated in an advisory board for the Metropolitan Economic Development Association (MEDA), and served various board positions with the St. Paul Chamber of Commerce. She is currently Board Chair of the Burnsville YMCA.

Cheryl holds a doctorate degree in educational psychology and counseling. She is a Registered Corporate Coach with the World Association of Business Coaches. Her dissertation was *A Descriptive Study of Mentoring From the Perspective of Mentors in Business and Industry*.

Acknowledgements

To my dear husband, Pat, who has patience beyond belief. When I announced I was semi-retiring from my leadership consulting business to simplify my life, he was a huge supporter. When I announced I would be writing this book and spending time supporting the success of woman-owned small businesses, he proclaimed, "How does this fit with simplifying your life?" Thank you for always being there no matter what new adventures I pursue.

To the editors of this book, Kate Leibfried and Mary Lager-Hagermeister. Thank you. I couldn't do it without you. You were instrumental in getting my words on paper and catching all the details.

To the beauty of my life, the lessons I have learned, the successes I have achieved, the joys and the tears that led me to this spot on my life path. I am grateful for the divine plan. The adventures continue.

Contents

Introduction: Not For Every Woman Entrepreneur...........................1

Stay CALM© and Build Your Business......................................7

Section C: Clarity and Simplicity

I Hear Voices...13

Is It Really a Risk?...17

What Will You Solve?...21

Keep it Simple, Stupid...27

Section A: Aim and Focus

Ladies, Start Your Engines...33

Where Are You Going?...37

You Can't Do Everything Online...41

Relationships Make it Happen..45

Selling is Not a Bad Thing...49

Section L: Leverage and Adjust

You Are Not an Imposter..57

On Being Superwoman...61

This Too Shall Pass..67

It Takes a Village...71

Section M: Measurements and Discipline

The Devil Is in the Details...77

Measure Twice, Cut Once...81

Be on Their Radar Screen..85

Making Money is Not an Option...89

What Are Your Business Lessons? 93

Section 2: The Stories

Angela Alvig 97

Suzanne Begin...101

Kelly Jahner-Byrne..105

Nancy Clairmont Carr..109

Charlotte Chipperfield..113

Julie Danskin...117

Brenda DeMotte..121

Char Dobbs..125

Julie Finch...129

Joan Gilles...133

Tera Girardin..137

Louise Griffith...141

Irmadene Hanson..145

Connie Hertz...149

Kathryn Hoy..153

Kristi Hughes...157

Carol Kaemmerer..161

Nicole Keirnes 165

Denise Krogman..169

Sarah Leitschuh..173

Michelle Mazzara..177

Patty McLain..181

Brenda Sterling Meyers..185

Cindy Moy...189

Paula Norbom...193

Cecelia Otto...197

Cathy Paper...201

Tara Peyerl..205

Amy Quale...209

Gwen Reidl..213

Margaret Smith...217

Angie Weber...221

Rev. Dr. Rachel Wetzsteon...225

AN INVITATION FROM CHERYL..229

Introduction

Not for Every Woman Entrepreneur

I never wanted a million-dollar business. When I started my business, my kids were ages two and six. I needed a flexible career that allowed me to have time with my children and stay involved in my professional passions and interests. Working for an organization would not give me the time and flexibility I wanted. Financially, I desired a comfortable income, but money was not the priority. My true aspiration was to help others and build a successful business—something I eventually did, but not without many twists in the road...

And So It Began...

I was the child of entrepreneurs. My parents owned their own business, starting the year I was born. Owning my own business has always been in my blood, and the family environment certainly supports the entrepreneurial desire.

I started my career in retail (Did I mention my parents owned a retail store? Oh, the impact those early years make on the future!). I worked for Dayton's Department Store in management and buying positions. There, I met the love of my life. While we were both still working at Dayton's, we got married and started a family.

My husband was offered a relocation, which meant I would no longer be able to work for Dayton's. I would be working for my husband which would have been a BAD idea. So, we relocated to Sioux Falls, South Dakota. I cried for weeks over leaving my job and moving. What in the world would I do in Sioux Falls, South Dakota?

Once we were settled into our new location, it was time for me to answer that question. I knew I loved mentoring others and had some definite ideas on what organizations could do to more effectively assist their employees with leadership and career development. The vision I had of what I could do became clear. Now, it was time to gain the skills I would need to make that vision a reality.

I decided to go back to school and earn my doctorate in psychology. I was able to convince the doctoral program to allow me to partner with the business school in researching and writing my dissertation on mentoring. After what seemed like an eternity (and a pound of flesh), I finished my doctorate and was ready to go.

We moved back to Minneapolis—St. Paul just after I finished my degree. I built a program, knocked on doors, and found several companies that were willing to take a chance on my "new" programs.

Starting a business was fun and exciting. Creating the plan, the products/services, and marketing were all strengths of mine. Getting enough work in the door was the challenge. How I wished someone would give me the key tips, help me with my sales process, support my dreams, open a door, or simply share in my ups and downs. There was nothing available that focused specifically on women entrepreneurs, so I created my own virtual mentoring team for my business through my networking connections. Their support was critical to my business success.

A key learning during that time was reaching out to others for support. I was about seven years into my business when one member of my virtual mentoring team pointed out to me that I was trying to be Super Woman by doing it all myself. What would happen if I asked a few of my key clients for referrals and support?

Following her guidance, I nervously reached out to one of my clients. Starting with an apology for even asking, I asked the question, "Do you know of others who might benefit from my work?" She responded with an enthusiastic "yes" and invited me to serve on a committee she chaired with the American Institute of Certified Public Accountants (AICPA). The task of this committee was to support retention of women in the profession and provide work/life balance tools to member firms. That opened door led me to speak and connect with organizations throughout the United States and Canada. This was a game changer for my business. The thing I remember most was her comment, "Cheryl, you always help me whenever I need it. It's about time you asked me to help you." That comment alone unlocked a door and assisted in the aim and focus for my business.

What's happening now...

Fast forward to today. I've run my own business for over twenty-five years. I have been blessed with opened doors and opportunities to work nationally and internationally. I have published five books. My business has supported the flexibility for raising my children and now spending time with my grandkids. Financially, my business has had highs and lows, but has generated the comfortable income I desired. While the journey has not always been easy, it has served my family and myself well.

About six years ago, women solopreneurs began to ask me the secrets to my success. I must admit I was a bit shocked to be asked. I wasn't aware I was a "success." The road was filled with ups and downs, dead ends and new beginnings, tears and joy. It was only when I began to mentor some of these women that I recognized the knowledge I had gained and the value I could be to their success. Just as in my consulting business, my work with women solopreneurs began small and grew from one woman to several to a mastermind group to a podcast to this book. I call this my "legacy work." This is my opportunity to pour into entrepreneurs all the knowledge, support, introductions, and intuition that I can to help them grow a successful, sustainable business.

I started the *Straight Talk for Smart Business Women* podcast in 2016. My vision was to create a venue for women small business owners to share their business journeys and key lessons they have learned. It was my mission to provide a platform for these women to expand their business presence and validate their journey. For the podcast listener, I wanted to provide practical tips and ideas, as well as validate their business journey and success.

As I listened to the stories shared on the podcast, it was clear to me that the lessons were similar. The stories and tips were rich with wisdom, regardless if the business owner was a new entrepreneur or a seasoned veteran. The messages were clear and needed to be shared with many. The stories are YOU! The lessons are for YOU! The opportunity for support, learning, and clarity is ripe for the taking.

One of my strengths is to see patterns in data. The podcast interviews were rich with data from entrepreneurs in the trenches of everyday business. The similar messages and lessons were clear as over a year of weekly episodes provided a source of wisdom to be shared with other women entrepreneurs.

These patterns have emerged into the **CALM**© model. The model identifies the components it takes to run, develop, and grow your entrepreneurial business. It is designed to create a path with wisdom and tools for your success. Through understanding this model, you can improve your knowledge, process, and actions. It is exactly the supportive tool I wish I had when starting my business not so long ago.

Why did I label this chapter "Not for Every Woman Entrepreneur?" This book may NOT be for you if you desire a quick fix or magic answers. This book may NOT be for you if you are not one to embrace tools and information for learning and growth. I recognize that you may need something different.

This book IS for you if you are passionate about what you do and want the support to bring your products, services, and talents to the world. This book IS for you if you enjoy following processes and formats to help build your success. This IS for you if you value the knowledge of those who have gone before you. And finally, this book IS for you if you are one to take action once you know where to head.

Stay Calm and Build Your Business

Have you ever suddenly realized something and knew it was an important idea or concept that needed to be shared? That is exactly what happened as I interviewed smart business women on the *Straight Talk for Smart Business Women* podcast. As they shared their business journeys and three key business lessons, I recognized the consistent messages in their interviews and the CALM© model was born.

The **CALM©** model was not built from theory. It was built from lessons, tools, and wisdom of women entrepreneurs in the trenches every day, working diligently to expand their message and grow their business. Each section of the model contains action items critical to build the foundations of your business.

The four components of the CALM© model are:

C – Clarity and Simplicity

A – Aim and Focus

L – Leverage and Adjust

M – Measurements and Discipline

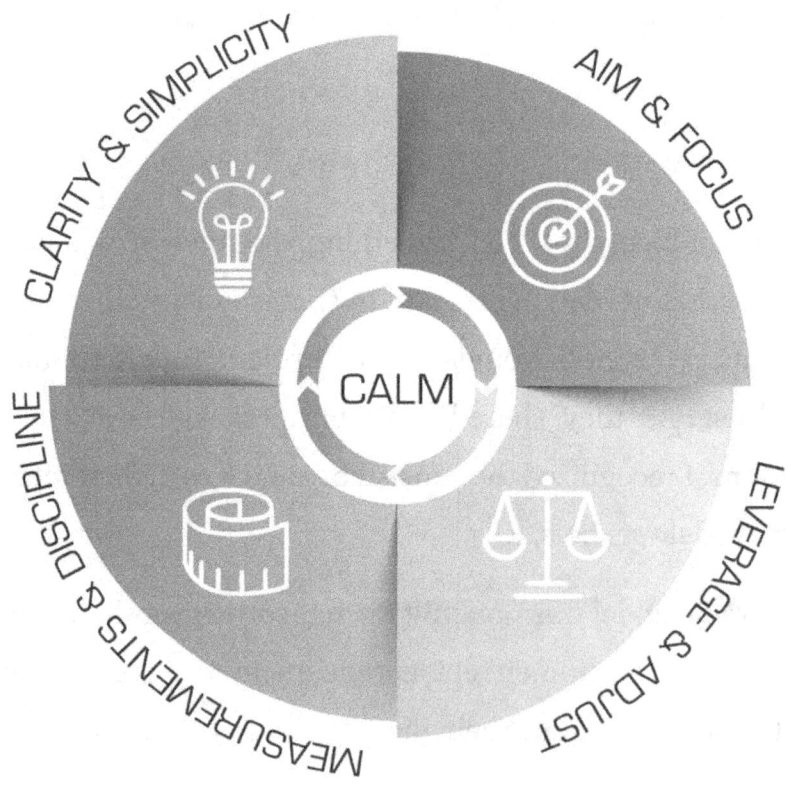

Clarity and Simplicity (C) is about creating a plan for your business that fits you, your reasons for developing this business, handling your inner critic, listening to your inner voice, and moving forward with confidence and clarity. We often over-complicate our business right from the start instead of focusing on building a strong foundation with the basic mission and message of the business. Think of this as the foundation of your business. Visualize a foundation of a home in construction. It looks rather boring. There is a cement structure with lots of dirt around it and a hole in the ground. Yet, the cement structure will support what comes next. Your clarity is important. The simplicity of your message will build a strong foundation and attract the clients/customers who need what you have to offer.

Aim and Focus (A) provides the fire to make it happen. It takes energy and drive to attract the relationships and network that will lead to selling and delivering your genius work. Aim and Focus is critical for managing your time, energy, and resources. Let's go back to our house example. Once you have the foundation, you can now build the structure. Aim and Focus requires awareness of how you will build your business. Focus is the energy you bring to do what is needed in creating this structure.

Your business will not grow unless you Leverage and Adjust (L). In your business, you are the center of the universe. As you build and grow, your confidence will grow. Your wisdom about you, your clients/customers, and their needs will grow. You will face challenges and lessons. You will face celebrations and joy beyond belief. These experiences and more allow you to create a successful, sustainable business. Think of this as how you will decorate each room of the structure you built as part of your Aim and Focus. Your personality needs to be a part of the decorating. The rooms you spend time in are another decision point. Do you need to be in all the rooms or are there others who can handle parts of your business? Leveraging your talents, building a support team, and handling the ups and downs of the journey are critical elements of the Leverage and Adjust components of the **CALM©** model.

All the creativity and passion in the world go out the window if the foundation of your business is not solid. Measurements and Discipline (M) are critical to keeping you on track. Without these, your business is a hobby and not a business to deliver your talents, tools, and products to the world. Think of this as the thermostat of your business. If the numbers are operating as intended, all will be well. If they are too high or too low, it indicates the need to make decisions and adjustments. Paying attention to the numbers that include (but are not limited to) financial indicators, can advise your strategies. Being disciplined in your business practices that contribute to sales and growth can be *the* challenge of an entrepreneur who loves to create and develop ideas.

Each of the following sections will enhance your understanding of the **CALM©** model and provide action steps. I recommend you review all the sections and then return to the areas that have the greatest needs and opportunities for you. As an entrepreneur, you will never be done. There will always be areas to expand, grow, and develop. The components of the **CALM©** model are not a checklist; rather, they are a continual guide to move your business from one level to the next.

Clarity & Simplicity

Create a plan for your business that fits you and your reasons for creating this business. Move forward with confidence, clarity, and simplicity.

I Hear Voices

Have you ever awakened in the middle of the night with an idea? Do you ever find yourself in the shower and think, "Should I do this?" We often ignore these messages or let life take over and set these voices aside. Often, these are voices of intuition that speak to your passions and purpose in your life or business. It is these voices that create the motivation and foundation of your business.

How did you know what business you wanted to start? Many of the women interviewed on the *Straight Talk for Smart Business Women* podcast described a "knowingness" that either came to them in a burst of inspiration, or entered their awareness gradually, years before starting their business. Some were afraid of taking the risk and remained uncomfortably silent and entrenched in their current job or career. Often a transition motivated them to take the first steps to start their business—a business that was haunting them and evolving in their head for years. They ignored their inner wisdom until they could no longer. The voice of purpose created the fire of motivation to step forward in their entrepreneur journey.

"The inner voice is what guides you to take inspired action despite the noise of daily life and all the stakeholders." Julie Dankin—one of my podcast interviewees—listened to that voice and stepped into a future that provided her pink Cadillacs and national recognition when her inner voices said "yes" to her Mary Kay adventure. Without the courage to listen to that voice in the beginning and all along the way, she would have never achieved the results and lifestyle she desired.

Char Dobbs of Char Style and Image Management Consulting moved from a career as an engineer to open her business as a style consultant. Did "stakeholders" around her question her decision? Of course! Did that stop her? It wasn't easy, but she listened to her inner voice and realized: "It's okay to be different and have a unique business model. Trust your gut." The faith in herself and willingness to listen has created unique marketing and business offers that set her apart from the rest.

You may be thinking, "This is crazy! What about all the aspects of a business plan? Don't I need all the questions answered before I begin?" My response is "yes" and "no." The seeds of your business start from you. The passion and focus build the foundation. The questions around marketing, brand, and finances springboard from that foundation. If you are the solopreneur, the foundation is you. Louise Griffith of One Shining Light says, "Honor your wisdom."

Cindy Moy of Hot Flash Sisters is a notable example of honoring her wisdom. She spotted a need that came from her own experiences and realization that something was missing. The inner voice was a force to be dealt with as she knew what was needed but had many missing pieces as to how to address the need. She states, "You don't need to have all the answers before you begin." The resources and plan emerged as she moved forward.

Action Steps For You

1. Whether you are in business one year, ten years, or thirty years, do you spend time listening to your inner voice?

2. When?

3. How?

4. What does it say?

5. How do you record, reflect, and process that information?

6. If you have ignored this inner voice, how will you honor it going forward?

Is It Really a Risk?

You have an obligation to bring your talents, ideas, and perspectives to the world. This is true whether you are employed by someone else or own your own business. Everything you say or do impacts the people around you and creates ripples in the world. We often think we don't have enough to matter but, trust me, you do have enough and your purpose does matter!

If you are an entrepreneur, your impact is of added importance. You have chosen to listen to that inner voice and stand out in the crowd through your unique business. Have you recognized that impact? The challenge as an entrepreneur is that there is no magic formula for understanding, articulating, and capitalizing on this impact. Sarah Leitschuh of Sarah Leitschuh Consulting, PLLC, advises that others may offer similar services but no one does it the way you do. "Accept your own process and avoid comparing yourself to others."

NO ONE can give you the formula to create the impact you will make if you follow your inner voice. The podcast guests have offered so many encouraging words that support this component of the model. Here are just a few of the quotes:

"Don't be afraid to say 'yes' to something you are not sure you do."
–Brenda DeMotte

"You don't need approval to take your own risks. Enjoy the ride and make use of your time and purpose in life." –Denise Krogman

"I don't have to be someone else's spokesperson to have a voice to be heard." –Carol Kaemmerer

"When the road less traveled doesn't work, create your own."
–Cecelia Otto

By now, you are probably nodding your head but asking, "How do you identify your area of impact?" Angie Weber, co-founder of Hello Life, identifies one of her key business lessons as, "You have to have a bigger 'why' to get through the challenges." Why are you creating this business? What will be the outcome for you? For others? For your business? The questions in the action steps are important as you create the clarity in your business.

Action Steps to Get to the Bigger Why

These action steps begin to point you in the unique direction for you and your business.

1. What transformations do you want to receive personally through your business?

2. What transformations do you want your clients/customers to experience as a result of engaging with your business?

3. What transformations would you like to see for your business because of delivering your products and services?

4. What transformations do you imagine possible because of your business?

5. Why are you the right person to deliver these products or services?

6. Why do you believe this business is important?

7. Why is NOW the right time for your business?

What Will You Solve?

So many entrepreneurs I meet spend hours designing programs and packages. They find joy in the creative process and think, "If this is what being in business is all about, I love it!" They then write flyers detailing all the great components of their genius work and wait for the phone to ring.

Eventually, they are not so thrilled with being in business because the phone is not ringing, money is not coming in the door, and they are met with a blank stare as others read their flyers, but do not quickly enroll. What's missing? Why are people *not* flocking to sign up? Everybody needs what you have developed, right?

My business was about three years old when I faced the same dilemma. I hired a marketing firm who proceeded to interview my clients and prospects to determine what was missing. They came back with two things. First, my clients and prospects didn't quite understand what I did. Second, if they did understand, they didn't need what I had. UGH! Talk about discouraged. After additional review of the interviews, it was clear that I was not speaking to what THEY needed. Instead, I was speaking to what I had created. Sounds simple, but it is a huge difference in how people understand you and your business.

Nancy Clairmont Carr of The Joy-Effect states, "Get up every day to learn and serve more." Learning and serving can be broad and general, or it can be focused on the clients/customers' needs and wants. By learning more about your clients/customers, you become clear on what issues they face and how you will solve their issues. The most creative programs and products will sit on shelves, never to be delivered, unless they solve a problem or issue for someone. This is an age-old and important question that drives the success of your business: "What problem does your business solve?"

My hunch is that your product or service is not meant to solve all issues for everyone. My hunch is that there is a certain ideal customer that will need your services. Start here. Picture the ideal customer in vivid detail. Next, survey or research those individuals. If you know people who fit this profile, ask them what issues they face, services they invest in, and how your products or services might help them. If you do not know specific individuals who meet the criteria of your ideal customer, you can ask others in your network for their opinions on the questions listed above OR you can ask them if they can identify people in their network who meet this criteria that you could interview. Ask them to make an introduction. Once you do, it will be much easier to fine-tune your resources to solve their problems.

Action Steps to Identify What You Solve

1. Who is the ideal client for your product or service? Be descriptive, including age and gender. What do they wear? What do they care about? Where do they shop? What do they do for fun?

2. List fifteen problems your product/services solve for your ideal client.

1.

2.

3.

4.

5.

6.

7.

8.

9.

10.

11.

12.

13.

14.

15.

3. List fifteen questions your product or service answers for your ideal client.

1.

2.

3.

4.

5.

6.

7.

8.

9.

10.

11.

12.

13.

14.

15.

4. Once you have completed the above steps, write one or two paragraphs:

a. Describe your ideal client and their issues.

b. List three to five key problems your product will solve.

1.

2.

3.

4.

5.

5. If you are unsure of how to best address your ideal customer's needs or wants, what strategy will you use to gather the research you need?

Keep It Simple, Stupid

I adhere to the simple wisdom of the KISS acronym: Keep It Simple, Stupid. Often, in our attempt to manage our own anxiety or provide something "perfect," we overcomplicate our business and stop the process of building, growing, and learning.

Angela Alvig of Simplify Wealth LLC states, "Be clear in your mind about what you bring and what you offer, but be willing to let your vision evolve." So far in the Clarity and Simplicity category we have focused on clarity. Now it is time to focus on simplicity.

If you listen to any great influencers, you will find that they share the same message over and over. They may tweak it a bit for different audiences, but the message is the same. As they learn more, they will add and adjust. The same is true for your business. You need to start with a simple message and allow it to evolve over time. Many business advisors and coaches advocate a business plan. I am not suggesting to *not* have a business plan, but I often find entrepreneurs become so buried with their plan's elements that they miss the essence of what they are doing, who they are targeting as their ideal client, and the simple message they must convey to bring business in the door. Many of the podcast interviewees echoed this sentiment:

  Nikki Keirnes of Keirnes Law states, *"Be flexible with your plan."*

  Michelle Mazzara of Luvafoodie states, *"Business plans are not set in stone."*

  Gwen Riedl of GROW Coaching and Consulting says, *"Be open, but focused and intentional."*

  Julie Dankin of Mary Kay states, *"Success as an entrepreneur is a total faith walk."*

Over the course of the four components of the CALM© model, you will have a living, breathing business path that is exactly that: a path, not a cement room. If you follow the action steps in the first three components of the Clarity and Simplicity section, you will have the start of your path.

I have heard many business advisors recommend that you create a business plan for your customers. I discovered that having a plan is for ME! It is designed to make business life less stressful and more focused. This, in turn, helps your customers, as you are better able to serve their needs. Julie Dankin states, "Vision conquers uncertainty, lack of direction, and attraction of customers." Grounding yourself in the path of your business will do all that and more.

Action Steps to Simplify Your Path

Take one sheet of paper and compile the lessons from the last three chapters into one document. The document should have three sections:

1. Why am I doing this business?

2. Who is my ideal client/customer?

3. What solutions will I provide to answer the needs of my ideal client/customer?

Refer to this sheet of paper whenever you need to return to the basic foundation of your business.

Aim & Focus

Attract the relationships and
network you need to sell and
deliver your genius work.

Ladies, Start Your Engines

"Whatever you do, get fired up about it." Joan Gilles of Financial Planning Partners wisely advises that you are the energy that sparks the engine of success for your business. If you can't get fired up about what you are doing, go back and visit the Clarity and Simplicity components of the CALM© model.

If you have truly defined how you wish to change the world, whom you wish to serve, and what problems you will solve, the "fired up" part will come easily.

But what happens on those down days? What do you do when you feel discouraged when the sale you thought would happen falls through? Louise Griffith of One Shining Light advises, "Take one more step." Stopping will not serve you or your business. Moving forward will keep the energy and business in motion. It will also give you a strong possibility that positive results will occur.

So that's the down days. What do you do on the up days? Most women entrepreneurs I meet are high achievers. In school, we wanted to always get the "A" and feel the achievement through the grade. While achieving is a positive driving force, it can also be the downside of being a high-achieving entrepreneur. We can't take our A's for granted and obsess about our B's and C's (Lord knows we'd never get D's or F's!).

Celebrate and cherish the A's. Celebrate and cherish the days when you hit the ball and it goes right where you want it to go. Bottle a piece of that celebration energy to grab onto when you are on the downside. Provide reminders to yourself of these special celebration days. I have a corner in my office where thank you notes and achievements are posted. Some are from clients. Some are sketches I make during those bright, sunny days.

What can you do during the days when the A's are not readily apparent? Kristi Hughes of The Fermented Experience starts her mornings by listening to or reading motivational messages or business strategies. This practice helps her create a "winners" mindset each day. Personally, I journal every morning and night, recognizing my intentions and gratitude in the morning and my "wins" for the day and what I am grateful for at night. These are simple steps to keep focused and moving forward.

Action Steps to Keep Fired UP

1. Create a "down day" plan. What can you do on those days to nurture your spirit? Post your plan in a key place so it is easy to access and remind you.

2. Make a celebration chart. List ten things you can do to celebrate on the day you have delivered what you desire for your business.

3. Create a celebration location to commemorate the thank you notes, achievements, and celebrations in your business.

Where Are You Going?

Now that your engine is started, let's go on a trip. What city should we visit? How will we get there? Will we fly? Will we drive? Take the back roads? Take the highways? Why did you choose the travel options you did?

You're probably wondering why I am asking you these ridiculous questions when you want to read about growing your business. These questions are similar to what you need to answer in deciding the Aim and Focus of your business.

First, where are you going? Do you want a solopreneur business or are you going to add employees? What are your financial goals? The aim component of your business takes the clarity component to another level by adding the clear descriptors of your business plan.

In my corporate coaching and consulting business, I started thinking everyone would want to hire me. While that may be true, it didn't help me with finding the right clients for my business. It was only when I defined my ideal client as Professional Service Firms (accounting, law, architecture, and engineering) that I could clearly identify where I was going and how I was going to get there. My aim was clearer. Then I was able to focus the actions I could take to move the journey down the road.

What actions did I focus on? First, I could clearly identify where to find these groups of people. Professional organizations exist for each of these groups. Easy, right? Well, not quite. I was faced with *many* options for targeting these groups, including:

- Joining the association and network
- Advertising
- Knocking on doors and providing a sales process
- Speaking
- Writing

While all of these were viable options, I needed to pair this with my talents and desires. I am not fond of just hanging out and networking. Advertising costs money, which I didn't have. I don't enjoy cold calling to find someone who would entertain a sales presentation. So, the best choice for me was speaking and writing. Every association looks for speakers and articles for their newsletters. This guided my strategy for business development and a sales process. After I identified the relevant associations, I researched the opportunities for speaking and processes for submitting articles for their publications. This research helped me fill in a calendar of action items that fit with the process for each organization.

My speaking and writing efforts were successful, which opened the door for business opportunities. This method of targeting potential clients may have been slower than knocking on doors and selling directly, but it was a process that fit my talents and motivation.

Can you see how identifying where you are going and how you will get there is critical to the Aim and Focus of your business? Once I became clear on where to aim, the choice of where to focus my time, energy, and financial resources became targeted and resulted in more business opportunities.

Action Items to Decide on Your Journey

1. You have already defined your ideal client. Where will you find them? If you cannot answer this question, review your description of your ideal client and develop a deeper description until you can identify a venue, organization, or avenue to reach these clients.

2. Once you have identified where you will find your ideal client, identify the options you have to reach them.

3. Of the identified options, which fit most closely with your talents? Choose at least one option as your strategy and develop an action plan for that strategy. If you are not sure, seek input from the ideal clients you interviewed back in the Keep It Simple, Stupid chapter.

You Can't Do Everything Online

Technology and social media can be a trap. We can become "busy" interacting on social media and develop the illusion that we are actually moving our business forward. In my podcast interview with Kathryn Hoy of UBS Financial Services, she reminded me, "You can't do everything on the internet." Yet, how many of us spend hours creating a social media plan or writing blogs or searching LinkedIn for new connections? It is not wrong to use technology to market your business, but when the focus becomes the internet and not relationships, we are missing the key reason why you created your business in the first place. Remember the transformation questions you answered in Chapter Four? Transforming you, your clients, and your business requires real-time connection to others.

Kristi Hughes of The Fermented Experience states, "Build relationships, not a website." Cindy Moy of Hot Flash Sisters echoes that sentiment in one of her key lessons, "Build a network and relationships." Many of the podcast interviews reinforced the importance of creating relationships in order to expand client reach.

How do you go about building relationships? There is a misconceived notion that you must be energetic and extroverted to build relationships. The goal in your network must be to meet everyone in the room at a networking event. Right? The one with the most business cards at the end of the night wins, right? Wrong! The best connections you can make are the ones where you and the other person connect on a personal level. This is important whether they are a networking connection or a potential client.

It only takes one valued relationship to open doors you can't even imagine could open. In my own business, I had a delightful client who accomplished many things because of our coaching. We completed our coaching relationships and several years went by. One day, she called and invited me to speak at an international conference. This one relationship led to the expansion of my practice to an international level.

It's not about quantity of relationships. It's about quality. How do you form quality relationships?

Actions to Develop Relationships

1.   Make a list of 100 people you know. Anyone? Yes, anyone. You need to shout about your business from the rooftops. Everyone you know should know what you are doing and how you will serve your ideal client.

2.   Identify those with whom you'd like to meet and start scheduling your meetings. Your goal is to meet with everyone on that list. The timeline will be impacted by how quickly business starts to develop and the time you have to conduct these meetings.

3.   Identify ten names from this list of 100 that you will meet with. Begin scheduling these meetings immediately. Your goal is to eventually meet with everyone on the list.

4. As you meet with these people, sort them into categories. I use the following designations:
- Key connection to support my business
- Possible connection to support my business
- Great person but not a connection to support my business

5. Develop a follow-up system for these groups. You are not the first person they think of when they wake up in the morning (surprise!). By having a follow-up system you can continue to provide useful information to both educate about your business and stay top-of-mind.

Relationships Make It Happen

Suzanne Begin of Begin Now! LLC has learned that, "Everyone in the whole wide world is a connection." She doesn't believe in sorting out "this one will be a client and this one won't." She knows she does not have the knowledge or insight to make that decision. Only the other person can make that determination. She also knows that, while someone may not be a potential client, they may know someone who is. By taking this attitude, she leaves herself open to new relationships.

Sarah Leitschuh of Sarah Leitschuh Consulting also "focuses on the relationship and adopts an attitude of abundance." She never knows if she will be a useful resource for the other person. Her goal is not to make a sale, but to create a relationship. She has found other entrepreneurs are sometimes fearful of competition and limit their connections due to this fear. Sarah recognizes that there is more than enough work for everyone in her profession. The right clients will come her way if she stays focused on the relationships.

"Be prepared as you might be surprised where business comes from" is one of the key messages from Gwen Riedl of GROW Coaching and Consulting. After several months of planning and implementing marketing plans, Gwen went back to review the sources of her business. To her surprise, many of the larger projects came from relationships with unexpected sources. A coffee meeting resulted in a large on-going contract. A chance meeting of someone she knew resulted in an on-going project. Being aware that you are always representing your work and creating new relationships is a key lesson for Gwen and the growth of her business.

Margaret Smith of UXL takes it one step further. In her podcast interview, she tells the story of attending a speaking event with a famous author and CEO. At the end of the speech she noticed that no one was speaking to him. She debated for a bit and decided, "Why not?" She approached him and offered him a copy of her book. Her advice is BE BOLD. "Being bold serves you well." Whether something will come of Margaret's boldness is unknown, BUT we do know nothing would have come of it if she hadn't reached out.

Actions to Expand Your Connections

1. What opportunities have you had to reach out to others and create new relationships in the last week?

2. Which of these opportunities have you taken advantage of?

3. Which of these opportunities have you let slip by?

4. How can you increase your relationship boldness in the next week?

Selling Is Not a Bad Thing

Why do many of us consider selling to be a dreadful thing? Why do we resist inviting people to become clients/customers and take advantage of the solutions we offer for the problems they face? We often avoid "selling" but one of the Aim and Focus goals of business is to generate revenue. Without revenue there is no business. Yet, many treat selling as an evil necessity.

I know for me, selling is hard because I don't want to hear "No." There is that uncomfortable silence while I feel totally and completely rejected. The discomfort was such a key factor for me for so many years that I avoided asking and waited for them to insist that we do business together before I would "accept" the sale. Crazy, huh?

Paula Norbom of Talencio says, "Selling has to be the primary activity of an entrepreneur." She's right. Without sales, you only have a hobby and not a business.

Let's take a step back even before the "selling" begins. Julie Finch of Finch Law says one of her critical business lessons was that, "You have to educate your market about your goods and services." She found she was even resistant to simply educating as it might seem too pushy. One of the lessons I learned through working with a marketing team many years ago is that clients have their own time tables. They may decide at any time that they'd like to invest in services such as mine and, if I'm not present at the time, they may choose someone else. This was a key "Aha!" moment and I recognized my "sales" process should be a continual education of the types of problems and solutions I can offer. To Julie's point, I learned that it was a good idea to keep my potential clients educated about my services until they were ready for my solutions, if ever. It was the first time that I developed a selling process that allowed relationship-building to be the Aim and Focus of my sales process.

Some of your connections will easily sign up and BOOM, you have moved to delivering services. Some relationships need you to follow up to help them decide. Another of Julie Finch's lessons is "follow up, follow up." I cannot tell you how many times I have met someone at an event, we have an enjoyable conversation, and I contact them later, asking a question or inviting them to get together. Crickets! Nothing! They never respond. OR they put me on their newsletter list, but never *actually* follow up. No relationship, no connection, no sale.

I am often asked, "How many times do you follow up?" My answer: "Until they tell you to go away." Everyone's life is busy. Just because they are not responding does not mean it is because of you. Jumping to that conclusion is not fair to them or you. You can coach people on how to say "yes," "no," or "not right now." I simply state in my personal conversation, email, or voicemail, "Feel free to tell me yes, no, or not right now. That way, I won't become a pest and can provide you with what makes sense for you." Your confidence and coaching will allow both of you to move forward with a positive relationship.

Eventually, you need to ask the question, "Do you want to do business with me?" I wish I had a magic, stress-free way to do this without triggering your rejection fears. Unfortunately, I don't have that magic readily at hand. I can, however, give you a few key tips that have helped me in asking this question:

  Start your meeting with a statement like, "I look forward to telling you more about my services. I find that my services are a great fit for some and not for others. I hope you will let me know if they are a fit for you, but I am completely OKAY if you find that they are not. Just let me know." This gives the prospect an expectation of giving you an answer. It keeps you away from convincing energy. Convincing energy is when you feel the pressure to force a choice on someone. Having to convince someone usually results in resistance. Once you start down the path of anxiety and pressure, both you and the client are in an ineffective communication pattern. Your permission upfront allows you to keep connected to the relationship and focus on educating about your product/service.

● The "no" answer is not a personal reflection about you. It is only a reflection of their current needs at this moment in time. By using my first tip, I find that it provides the opportunity to open the discussion at a later time.

● "No" does not mean "no forever." Ask if they would be open to continued communication about your services in the future.

● I have found some of my best referral sources are individuals who said "no," but saw the fit for others and actively sent them my way. I encourage you to add to your discussion a reminder that your business grows from referrals; if they find someone whom they think would be a fit, you would appreciate the introduction.

Actions for Your Sales Process

1. How do you make new relationships?

2. How do you learn about them?

3. How do you tell them about you and your business?

4. How do you continue to educate them on your business solutions?

5. How do you invite them to be a client/customer?

6. How do you follow up and keep a relationship with them?

CALM

LEVERAGE & ADJUST

Leverage & Adjust

Learning and growing. Success and failure.
Challenges and opportunities.
The entrepreneurial path is always creating
opportunities to Leverage and Adjust.

CALM

LEVERAGE & ADJUST

You Are Not
an Imposter

Perhaps you have heard of "imposter syndrome." This concept describes individuals who are marked by an inability to internalize their accomplishments and a persistent fear of being exposed as a "fraud."[1] There are two times during the year that I can predict my corporate consulting will be slow: August and December. The phone will not ring. Clients will not return calls. Emails will slow down. Despite being in business for over

---

[1] "Imposter syndrome," *Wikipedia*, last modified December 15, 2017. https://en.wikipedia.org/wiki/Impostor_syndrome.

twenty-five years, when these times come, you will hear me say, "That's it! They've discovered I don't know what I'm talking about." My husband always laughs and completely ignores my unfounded fear.

We are all prone to moments of imposter syndrome, but we do not need to stay in that unfounded fear. If you do, your business will also be stuck in fear. Many of the podcast interviews focused on this exact topic and solutions to move past this uncertainty. The topic of knowing and using your strengths was loud and clear in many of the interviews. Many used the StrengthsFinder assessment for getting to know and manage their strengths and talents. Joan Gilles of Financial Planning Partners sums it up when she states, "Know your strengths and ignore your weaknesses." When you understand your strengths and how you best operate, you also know what can throw you off course. For me, I thrive on being active and borderline stressed out. When things slow down and I don't have problems to solve, I make problems to solve. Crazy, huh? By knowing this, I don't allow the semi-annual imposter syndrome meltdowns to take over my ongoing moods and slow me down.

Additionally, knowing your strengths and weaknesses can help you decide what to delegate, who you need on your support team, and how to set the business so it honors who you are. While Joan advises to "ignore your weaknesses," my suggestion is to honor your weaknesses. They will not go away, but they can help you decide where to invest in your business to play to your strengths. For example, I am a good writer, but terrible at details. Without delegating the editing for this book, you would easily find typo after typo that I missed.

Tera Girardin of Tera Photography focused on this area during much of her podcast episode. "Run your own race" is one lesson she has found for herself in running a successful growing business. There are so many times we compare ourselves with others and are told what we "should" be doing. When you use others as your measuring stick, you tend to feel inadequate, like an imposter. Tera advises, "Always honor how you work and create schedules that work for you." When she stays true to who she is, the business works for her and allows things to "float and flow," the energy and joy remain strong and so does her business.

Keeping track of your mindset and your energy is another component of staying out of imposter syndrome and staying grounded in the strengths you bring to your business. When your mindset is guided by fear or you lose track of why you are in business, you become more susceptible to imposter syndrome. Julie Dankin of Mary Kay knows from her own success that, "Your current mindset grows your life and your business." Awareness, acknowledgement, and support through your own internal gifts, talents, and messages are the keys to moving past fear and into possibilities.

Action Steps to Monitor Your Mindset

1. If you have taken the StrengthsFinder Assessment, take it out and review. What are your strengths? Your blind spots?

2. If you have not taken StrengthsFinder or any other assessment, you may find it a missing component to understanding and managing your strengths and opportunities. You will find the StrengthsFinder assessment if you purchase the book *StrengthsFinder 2.0* by Tom Rath.[2] Access to the assessment is included in the purchase.

---

[2] Rath, Tom. *StregthsFinder 2.0.* New York, NY: Simon and Schuster, 2013.

On Being Superwoman

Raise your hand if you can leap tall buildings with a single bound. Raise your hand if you THINK you can leap tall buildings with a single bound. Yes, I thought so! You THINK you can, but physically can't. I often see this in women entrepreneurs. We think we can do it all, but in reality, we can't.

I'm not saying you shouldn't dream big or set ambitious goals. What I am saying is you need a team of support people to assist in "the leap." As Julie Dankin states, "The entrepreneur challenge is to wisely delegate." I remember thinking, "How can I delegate? I have no money to hire anyone!" It was only after I realized that *delegating* didn't necessarily mean *hiring an employee* that I began to explore ways to build a virtual support team. Margaret Smith states, "Don't think it all has to be created by you, or you need to do it all yourself."

The first step is to recognize what you need or want to delegate in order to leverage the highest and best use of your time and talents. In the previous chapter, we discussed knowing your strengths. It would be simple to give you a list of what to delegate, but it would be *my* list and not *yours*. You come with a set of strengths, talents, and desires that tell you where to spend your time. For example, you love the creative work, but the financial aspect of your business creates more stress than you can imagine. Or, for me, I am great at strategic thinking and designing programs to meet my client needs. I am terrible with details. In both examples, I hope you can see the obvious components that can, and should, be delegated.

Amy Quale of Wise Ink Publishing understands the use of delegating to not only manage her business, but also create balance in her life. She says, "Try to manage the flow and all the business demands through effectively delegating." Brenda DeMotte of Professional Counseling & Grief Services, Inc. & Grief Demystified states, "You can have balance!" She discusses in her podcast episode the importance of knowing and managing the realities of your business and your personal capabilities.

The two reasons I hear for not delegating are 1) Not knowing *who* to delegate to and 2) limited funds. Let's address the "who." There are so many small businesses out there with capabilities to serve what you need once you have identified your delegation needs. I have five virtual assistants. Why five? They all provide different talents and capabilities. I know who to tap into based on what the project needs. I have referred other entrepreneurs to resources that handle monthly financials and billing or managing social media marketing. There are resources out there once you are clear on what you need.

Margaret Smith of UXL is amazing at delegating and finding resources. She uses neighborhood high school and college students. Her work requires her to put together reports and she can access assistance right next door. Think broadly and consider what resources might be out there.

Item number two is limited funds. I get it! If you get in the habit of budgeting a certain dollar amount for delegation services, you will circumvent the "I'll wait until I have the money" fallacy. Could you spend $50 per month? $100? $200? Where could you start? It is amazing how starting with even two to three hours per month of virtual assistance can save you stress and increase your effectiveness, as well as your sales.

There are, however, things you should NOT delegate, at least when you are small. The two areas I believe you need to keep as your duties, no matter how challenging, are financial oversight and sales.

Financial oversight does not mean you need to write the checks. What it does mean is you need to review your financial situation monthly. Where are the expenses? Are invoices being paid promptly? Where should you invest more time or money? No one can make those decisions for you.

Sales must stay with you until you are large enough to hire sales people. Even then, sales is a primary role for the entrepreneur. No one knows your business like you do or is better equipped to speak about the solutions you provide. Relationship-building and the sales process are roles you cannot leave to others. Early in my business, I hired a telemarketing firm who guaranteed they would get me appointments with companies to learn about my business. I gave the rep fifty names. Not one appointment was set. After we parted company, I called ten of the names on the list and landed four appointments. This turned out to be an expensive and eye-opening example of trying to delegate something that needed to be owned by me.

Through this experience, I learned how important it is to hire someone to represent my business that can speak my language and who is in alignment with my brand. This includes not only sales representatives, but writers for your blog, social media, and website copy. Unless you can find the "mini me" voice, the activity should remain with you.

Actions to Delegate

1. If money were not an obstacle, list the ten things you would NOT do so you could spend more time with what you love to do.

1.

2.

3.

4.

5.

6.

7.

8.

9.

10.

2. Seek referrals for virtual assistants and resources by asking others, "Who do you know that does_____?"

3. Start small and realistic, but start! The list of ten things can give you focus on what to delegate and how to leverage your strengths to optimize your time and energy. Anything that potentially frees up time and allows you to put your strengths to use should be considered, even if it is a small step.

This Too Shall Pass

Tara Peyerl decided to return to corporate work after her entrepreneurial experience. Cindy Moy describes the challenge of taking off on her entrepreneurial concept, only to realize how much she didn't know. Rachel Wetzsteon discusses her uncertainties of business focus and revenue that resulted in breakthroughs in her business. There are so many stories in the *Straight Talk for Smart Business Women* podcast of facing challenges and moving on. Tenacity and resilience are clear messages in learning to Leverage and Adjust in your business.

Here are key quotes from the *Straight Talk for Smart Business Women* podcast interviews:

Tara Peyerl: *"There will always be mountains to climb, but remember setbacks aren't fatal."*

Joan Gilles: *"Learn from mistakes because you will make them."*

Cindy Moy: *"There will always be more lessons."*

Brenda DeMotte: *"Don't kick yourself for making the wrong decisions."*

Julie Finch: *"You just need to be comfortable being uncomfortable."*

Rachel Wetzsteon: *"There might be a breakdown before the breakthrough."*

Now that you've read their advice, are you sure you want to continue this entrepreneurial path? I don't write this to discourage you, but to have you feel and understand the resilience you'll need on this path. You'll inevitably encounter hardships while you are trying to deliver your passions, products, and services to others. There are times when I have failed or felt discouraged, but kept moving forward. From these challenges, I gained powerful lessons that have helped grow and strengthen both myself and my business.

Connie Hertz of Living in the Glow proclaims, "Never quit." Suzanne Begin of Begin Now! LLC shares, "Experience is important." With experience comes confidence, wisdom, and strength in your path and the foundation of your business.

Cece Otto of An American Songline describes in her podcast episode a business project where everything that could go wrong, did go wrong. Telling the story years after what could have been a disaster, she recalls the lesson she learned: "Embrace grace in the moments of chaos." Sounds simple, but it's not easy.

You have a way of being resilient. *You* have a way of embracing grace in the moments of chaos. It is uniquely yours. Have you identified it?

Sometimes the challenge is intense or lasts a long time. What do you do then? What is your resilience plan? For me, it is stepping back when things are crazy and breaking the tension. Massages, meditation, friendship, and journaling are all contributors to my resilience. The excitement of being an entrepreneur is that frustrations can crop up or disappear in an instant. Just when I start to despair that I won't have any new business, three new projects show up in one day. It is what keeps me curious and excited to work in and on my business each day—you never know what that new day will bring.

Action Items for Resiliency

1. Think of a time you have experienced a setback or challenge.

2. Identify the factors that helped you to move on and eventually heal from the hurt or challenge of that situation.

3. What can you use as a reminder to yourself when setbacks or challenges occur? Call this your Resiliency Recovery Plan. Keep it near! Don't lose it. You never know when it will be exactly what you need to keep your business on the path.

It Takes a Village

"Create a support team inside and outside your business," states Nancy Clairmont Carr of the Joy-Effect.

Most women business owners and professionals I have met or worked with over the years tend to think they can do it better, faster, and more effectively if they do things on their own. While it may be true in some cases, it will not create the energy and support you need to take your business to the next level.

Irmadene Hanson tells the story in her podcast episode of joining every networking venue she could when she first started her business. She quickly identified that some groups simply drained her energy. Other groups challenged her and she felt motivated by the interactions. She recognized that she needed other business women who were smarter or more advanced in their businesses to challenge and support her to do the same.

Denise Krogman also discusses the "right" networking groups to join. If the individuals around her were not positive or did not listen, she knew they were not the right advisors for her. Cathy Paper of RockPaperStar knows that asking others for advice and building strong relationships continues to support and grow her business.

Angie Weber of Hello Life knows she could not have launched her business or experience the successes she has had without having the right support system in place.

Hopefully, you are nodding your head as you read the sage advice from each of the entrepreneurs listed above. But, how do you know who to choose or how to discern the "village" you need? Here are a few criteria:

- Are they positive?
- Do they listen?
- Do they challenge you?
- Are some at business levels beyond where you are now?
- Do they give you advice, but respect what you choose even if it is not their advice?

Where do you find them? The village may include hired coaches, mentors, or business consultants. They can also be individuals you meet at networking events with whom you find a connection and wish to support each other's businesses. There is not one place to look. If you are intentional in seeking your village of supporters, you will find them. Regardless of paid or unpaid, the criteria list is the same.

Actions to Build Your Village

1. Take an inventory of your current support team. Include the following categories:

a. Friends and family
b. Trusted peers
c. Coaches – those who advise and challenge
d. Mentors – those who advise, challenge, and protect
e. Advocates – those who open doors for opportunities

NOTE: You will likely have more names in the friends and family and trusted peers group than the advocates and mentors categories. That is fine. It is the awareness that is key.

2. If you have no one in the advocate and mentors group, set an intention to seek individuals to fill these roles. Who might be an appropriate fit? Do you need to expand your relationships? Can others help you find these relationships?

3. Focus your attention on asking for and seeking these individuals in networking groups, peers, friends and family, or even past clients. Once you focus your intention and attention in this direction you will be amazed by who might show up.

Measurements & Discipline

Without a foundation, the house of cards tumbles. Processes, operational tools, regular and consistent marketing, and tracking the numbers are critical components of a successful business.

The Devil Is In the Details

This section is probably my least favorite. I would much rather work with clients, develop products, create relationships, learn, and grow. I hate the details of running a business. Yet, if I don't pay attention to them, who will? Yes, I can hire things out, but ultimately it is my business and the success or failure rests with me. As the saying goes, "The buck stops here."

Angela Alvig of Simplify Wealth sums it up nicely, "Work 'on' your business, not just 'in' your business." Michael Gerber, in his book *The E-Myth*[3], also echoes that thought. He cautions entrepreneurs that not paying attention to key business details can result in business failure. He identifies many key business details. Some of these include financial management, marketing strategy, and customer retention and satisfaction. Start from day one of your business with creating the measurement dashboard. It need not be complex (remember, Keep It Simple, Stupid), nor does it need to take a great deal of time. I find a monthly review of key items is all that is needed in my business.

So, what should you be monitoring? Here is a list of what I believe every business needs on their dashboard:

1. Finance

    a. Are you profitable?

    b. Can you pay yourself?

    c. Are your clients paying?

    d. Are your accounting records processed and up-to-date?

2. Process and Procedures

    a. Do you have standard operating procedures for your business?

---

[3] Gerber, Michael. *The E-Myth Revisited: Why most small businesses don't work and what to do about it.* New York, NY: HarperCollins, 2004.

b. Are they documented?

c. Is there anything you can delegate at this point?

3. Information Technology (IT)

a. Is your technology working properly?

b. Is your website working properly?

c. Do you need updated security?

4. Marketing

a. What marketing efforts have you employed in the last month?

b. What are the results of your marketing efforts?

If you were to work for a larger organization, they would have all this and more in place and handled by a team of people. Just because you are small, doesn't mean these factors don't exist in your business. They do and someone needs to pay attention. That would be you.

Action Plan to Address Your Business Needs

1. Start tracking the items identified in this chapter's list. Add other areas of consideration as indicated by your specific business needs.

2. Adjust your strategies as needed, based on your review. For example, if you are not profitable, do you need to adjust your pricing structure? Another example: you are running a marketing campaign with great results. Evaluate what is working well so you can duplicate this in future campaigns.

3. Identify actions you will take in the next month based on the results of this review.

Measure Twice, Cut Once

Many years ago, my husband decided to install a shower door in one of our bathrooms. He measured and cut all the pieces and then started to install the door. Lo and behold, he had made an error in measuring the top track. It was too short! There was no way to fix the error as the cut had been made. As he stood there in disgust, he wisely stated, "I should know better. Measure twice, cut once."

The "measure twice, cut once" message has stuck in my head as an application to my business. I have spent many dollars on training, consultants, brochures, and the latest social media that, in hindsight, should never have been spent. There were times when paying for these services created overwhelming credit card debt, which caused stress and moved me off focus. If I had only taken extra time to "measure twice," I would have decreased my stress and financial investments.

Am I the only one who looks for the next shiny object or magic answer to catapult my business to the next level? I wish that were the case. Over and over I see entrepreneurs spending without thinking through the need for the investment OR I see entrepreneurs hesitating to spend on items that will support sales. Irmadene Hanson of Magnify Your Influence states, "Spend dollars on the right things at the right time." What does that mean? You need to intentionally and wisely consider what you can afford and what can make the greatest impact for the next step of your business. If you are not sure, or this is not a strength for you, call in your support "village" to advise you.

Four critical questions I ask when deciding on investing are:

- Will it generate revenue?
- How will this added support build long-standing relationships?
- Will it free my time to spend on marketing and sales?
- How many dollars can I invest in my business right now, without creating a burden?

Undercapitalization can be the downfall for many entrepreneurs. A key lesson Kristi Hughes of The Fermented Experience learned was, "Don't wait to ask for capital." A banker is a key advocate for you and your business. Make sure you have the right one who understands and supports your business. If the one you have doesn't fit this role, interview until you find one that does.

Walt Disney was denied by 302 banks for a loan to start Disney because he "lacked originality."[4] Early in my business, I decided to apply for a small business loan. Three banks told me "no" before one bank listened to my story and supported my loan. Banking is fickle. Find a bank that understands and supports your vision and growth.

Action to Create Your Business Investment Plan

1. Identify all the investment considerations you have for your business. This might include websites, support people, coaches, consultants, training, etc.

---

[4] *Get It Done Transportation*. Facebook. December 12, 2012.
https://www.facebook.com/GetItDoneTransportation/posts/388555694562307

2. Prioritize your considerations. If you are not sure, find an advisor to help you. This should be someone who receives no benefit or impact from your decision. For example, a spouse is impacted by your financial decisions. A potential coach is impacted by your financial decisions. A small business accountant would be a neutral source who would not be impacted by your financial decisions.

3. Identify the budget you can reasonably afford for investing in your business next year.

4. Set forth a six-month plan for investing based on the priority and the budget. Trust that the other items will happen when the timing and budget fits.

CALM

MEASUREMENTS & DISCIPLINE

Be On Their Radar Screen

Measurements and Discipline is important beyond the financial sales and operational considerations of your business. It also applies to how you think about and attend to the relationships in your business.

Many years ago, I hired a marketing firm to help me understand why I was not making more sales. Everyone needs my services, right? They are the best, aren't they? Why doesn't everyone sign up as soon as they hear about me? As I worked with this firm, it became clear to me that the timing on when they purchased was based on their needs, not mine (profound, huh?). This required me to shift my "sales now" mindset to one of "be on their radar screen." When the timing was right for them, I wanted them to think about me as an option.

The shift to regular, disciplined communication had a direct connection to my phone ringing with the right clients seeking my expertise. This switch in mindset led me to establish a regular, disciplined communication process that included all my contacts as well as targeted individuals. Let me give you a brief example of how this worked. For all of my connections, I provided daily motivations and monthly newsletters. For targeted individuals, I had a client management system to contact them personally once every three to six months. When I strayed from this discipline I would recognize the drop in new projects very quickly. When I remained true to this practice, the revenue and project stream remained consistent. How did I know? I had the measurements in place to monitor this process.

Kathryn Hoy, of UBS Financial, echoes this strategy when she advises, "Have a service model of regular, disciplined communication with your customers or clients." She does not believe this is an internet-based process if you wish to truly have a trusted relationship that builds and grows your connections. Nothing can replace human contact.

Another area of discipline is how you handle your networking and relationship-building process. Kelly Jahner-Byrne is the role model of creating strong, valued relationships. One of the critical items she stresses is, "Follow-up is key." How many times have you met someone, taken a business card, and sat at your desk wondering what to do with the new connection? The discipline of connecting is important to continuing the relationships needed to build and grow your business. Ask yourself: How can you help this person? What do they need that you can provide? Don't just sell your services, but truly support their needs.

The final mandatory area in your review of your disciplined process is asking for referrals. When I ask entrepreneurs where their business comes from they say, "Referrals." When I ask how they ask for referrals, they give me a blank stare. A referral request plan is another discipline process. When do you ask? How do you ask? Can you simply build it into your regular conversations? Something like: "My business grows from referrals. If you know of someone who could use XYZ, I hope you will think of me and send them my way." Believe it or not, most people don't even think about how they can support your business unless you ask. Some of my best referral sources are people with whom I have never done business, but are clear about my business, my ideal clients, and my appreciation of referrals.

Action Steps For Client Relationships

1. Do you have regular, disciplined communication with your current and past customers/clients? Do you know what you will say when you ask for the referral? Having a written script can often ease the discomfort of asking.

2. Do you have a referral request process? Is it communicated with every relationship you make in your business? This does not involve payment of fees. The request is merely asking the question, "Do you know anyone who might benefit from my services?"

Making Money Is Not an Option

Making money is not an option. Making money is a requirement. If you are not making money, do you really have a business?

As I reflect on the podcast episodes that contributed to this book, not one of them questioned their being in business. Not one of them had their foot half in and half out. They were "all in." Yes, some had to refocus as they learned what was working and what was not. Some found that their vision and the services they offered did not meet what the market would buy. They reformatted, refocused, and moved forward.

As Julie Dankin said in her episode, "Being an entrepreneur is a total faith walk." Your belief, clarity, and energy move you forward, believing in the services or products you offer.

I'll say it again: Making money is not an option. Making money is a requirement. You deserve to receive value in return for the value you provide to others. The value equation includes money. Many women entrepreneurs are often apologetic for charging for their products or services. They worry that their pricing is too high. I often say, "Set your fee and then double it. That is what you should be charging." Now, what mindset do you need to get comfortable with that number?

Making money is not an option. Making money is a requirement. Have I said that already? Have you heard it? One of the areas you cannot delegate is the financial monitoring of your business. Sure, you can delegate paying bills or sending invoices, but you cannot delegate the overall financial picture. Without the discipline to attend to the finances, your business ownership is not complete. If you don't understand, don't enjoy, or don't know what to do, seek help from an advisor who understands your business. Having a small business accountant on your team is a good place to start.

What happens when you reach your financial goals? Do you stop growing and remain stagnant? Do you expand and hire a team? My response is to go back to the C component of the CALM© model: Clarify and Simplify. What are the new voices telling you? What makes sense for you and the lifestyle you wish to create?

For me, I started as a solopreneur and established a financial base. I decided to add employees and quickly learned how miserable I was managing other people and not being on the frontline with client service delivery. It did not take long before I disassembled the team and returned to my solopreneur status.

Action Plan to Monitor the Money

1. Do you monitor the financial picture of your business on a monthly, quarterly, and annual basis?

2. Looking at your financial picture, what is your plan of action? If you're operating at a profit, what are your next steps? If you operate at a loss, what will you do?

3. What financial advisors do you need to responsibly manage your business?

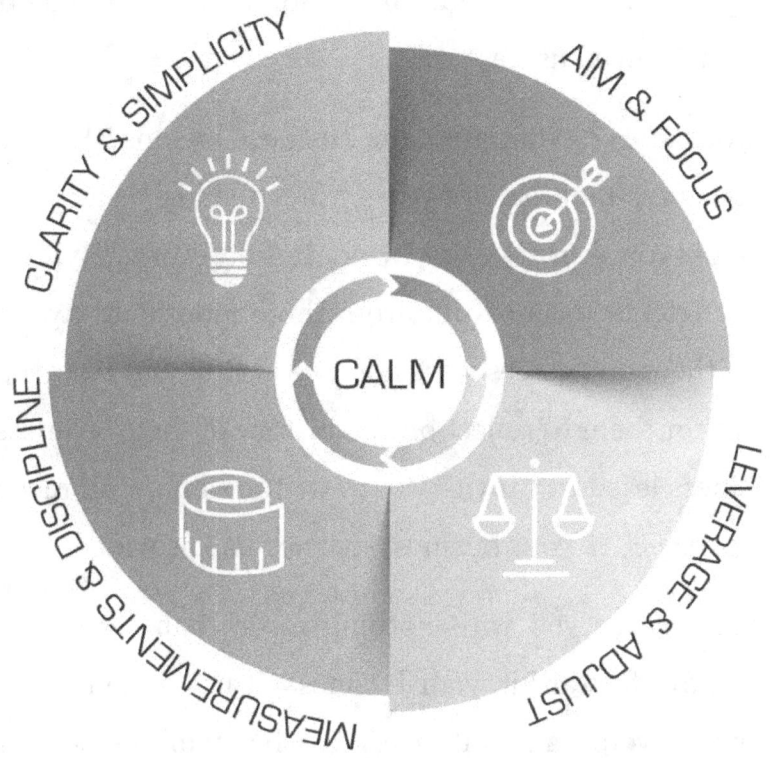

What Are Your Business Lessons?

Every *Straight Talk for Smart Business Women* episode is a story filled with information for *you*. Some of these entrepreneurs are just starting. Some have been in business a long time. They all share the same journey of desire to bring their passion, talents, and wisdom to others and do it on their own terms, in their own business.

What is your story? What are your business lessons? Even if you have only been in business months, not years, you still have a story and probably multiple lessons you learn every week, if not every day. The podcast interviewees ranged in business life from three months to twenty years, or more. Many of the interviewees were nervous at first, but later reported how powerful it was for them to reflect on the history of their business and their three key business lessons. I invite you to do the same. Embrace the power, wisdom, and perspective your business journey has provided.

If this book leaves you with nothing more than a tool, a tip, or an inspiration to move forward in your business, it has done its job. Enjoy the ride and the power your path embraces. I wish you all the best as you move forward in your business journey. In the meantime, keep growing your business!

For access to the podcasts as well as additional tools, resources, and support, visit my website:
www.CherylLeitschuh.com

-Section 2-

The Stories

In April, 2016, I decided to start the ***Straight Talk for Smart Business Women* Podcast.** My vision was to have a venue for women small business owners to share their business journeys and key lessons. It is my mission to provide a platform for these women to expand their business presence and validate their journey. My vision for the listener is to learn tips, ideas, and to affirm their business journey and success.

The participants I choose for the podcast are all female small business owners who are...

- Passionate about owning their business
- Committed to building their business

Courageous enough to take action while learning and growing both personally and as an entrepreneur

After sixteen months of weekly shows, it was clear to me that the messages and lessons of these courageous women shared common themes—vital themes that needed to be shared on a larger platform. The ***Straight Talk for Smart Business Women*** book was conceived and the **CALM©** model emerged.

The following section is a recap of each smart business women who contributed their lessons to this book and the CALM© model. The section for each contributor is a high-level recap of the podcast episodes. They are meant to capture the essence of the episode, but cannot capture the depth and personality of the individual. For that, you will need to access the podcast episode. You will also see similar lessons and messages among the stories. It is that duplication and consistency that led to the creation of the CALM© model.

I hope you will read the overviews, internalize the lessons that will benefit your business' growth, and validate your own personal journey. If a particular entrepreneur or lesson resonates with you, you can access the interview and hear more. The podcasts are available on iTunes, Google Play, Spotify, and Stritcher, as well as my website: www.CherylLeitschuh.com.

Angela Alvig

Simplify Wealth

"I took a leap of faith and jumped in with both feet."

After years of serving as a CPA and family office business manager, Angela decided to head in a new direction and start a personal CFO company called Simplify Wealth. She had the technical expertise, but was unaware of the process needed to create an entrepreneurial business plan. On her journey, she has discovered it is just as important to build her personal entrepreneur leadership skills as well as her technical expertise.

Transitioning from the corporate world to entrepreneurial business was a process riddled with surprises and challenges. Angela was willing to tackle these new learnings to launch, build, and grow her business by setting realistic goals to focus and personalize her services. First steps included analyzing her time and knowing the level of service she wished to provide.

That gave her insight to know what she could and could not realistically deliver.

Angela's unique business model gives her the role of a family or personal CFO. She coordinates the wealth and personal needs of high net worth individuals. She is not a CPA or financial advisor; rather, she coordinates these services to ensure her clients are receiving all they need in the complex world of financial management. Because her hybrid model is unique, she received many naysayers early on. Nevertheless, she knew she saw a void in the market and she had the courage to move forward. By the time she was ready to have the "road show" and meet with others, she had developed an understanding of her prospective clients' needs and was met with a positive response.

Angela's Advice ...

Be clear about what you do and who you serve, but be flexible

Clarity allows you to say "yes" to the work that fits for you. However, being too rigid will not allow you to create what is needed for the "right" clients. As Angela's business evolves, she has come to see the opportunity to add services based on her clients' needs.

Be authentically you

Being confident in who you are and what you offer is important. Clients then become comfortable and buy "you." As a solopreneur, that confidence in yourself builds trust. You won't get too far if you try to be something you are not. If you don't like your client and they don't believe in you, the work will be difficult, to say the least.

Work *on* your business, not just *in* your business

It is easy to focus on email or expand your technical knowledge. It won't build your business. Things like newsletters, marketing, or social media can be outsourced to get it done and build your business.

Hire a coach like you would a personal trainer. You, as the business owner, need to make the decisions, but stepping back from the business to decide where to focus is important. That is the value of a coach.

When deciding what to outsource, check with friends, family, and others you know. Start with your network and see how you can help others build their business as you build yours.

Don't be afraid to ask others to help

Whether you're looking for new clients or business support, people are always willing to help if you ask. Every connection is important. Be curious because you never know how a new relationship could help you build your business.

Simplify Wealth LLC

Angela works with clients as their Family or Personal CFO, providing focused, independent, "family office" services. Her firm, Simplify Wealth, provides financial coordination and concierge/personal assistant services to its family office clients.

www.simplify-wealth.com

Suzanne Begin

Begin Now!, LLC

"I watched good people leave their souls in organizations."

Suzanne had a thirty-year career in corporate and nonprofit management. As an executive leader and coach, she has played a prominent role in several organizations. When she started her business, Begin Now!, LLC, she took that career experience and applied her knowledge to help others.

One year into her business, she has focused on bringing love into the world by marrying the talents and souls of the people whom she serves. Through Suzanne's coaching, training, and consulting work, she brings hope to many and empowers her clients with a sense of a higher purpose so that they can start expressing themselves in the world NOW.

Suzanne's Advice ...

Be sure to know who you are and who you are gifted to be

We can all be so many things. What you are NOT is just as important as what you are. When you start in business, you may be tempted to take on work to pay the bills. The trouble with this is that you really are not impacting the world as much as you could.

It's critical to stay grounded and focused on who you are. Have a group of support people to keep you honest. Colleagues and support teams will push and prod you to be true to yourself and expand who you are. You can't do this on your own. Others need to be your mirrors.

Another idea is to have an accountability partner to run things by so you ensure your thinking is in alignment. Just because you own your company doesn't mean you need to be alone.

Valuing your experience is important

Many of us walk through life unconsciously carrying on as if we are drones. You need to be intentional in everything you plan in your business—

from the website to marketing. Experience must be in the foreground and not an afterthought.

Put your client's experience and gifts first. If you understand your clients, you will know how clients will experience their connection to everything you do. What do people experience when they see your website? It is not the words, it is the emotion they feel when they interact with you and your resources.

Everyone in the whole wide world is a connection

If you are clear about who you are, know who you are in the world, and value the experiences of others, then everyone you meet is a valuable connection. Sometimes we are so concerned with selling that we forget the connection. The next person you meet could be a new client, a referral, or something even more. It may take time to know where the new connection may take you.

You need to find a way to meet people and keep it all in balance. Set aside time for different connections in your life. How much time do you devote each week to you? To friends? To new connections? When the schedule is full this week, don't get "weirded out" about it. Simply schedule when you can. Appointments will happen when they are meant to occur.

Think connections, not network. Networks are what you use to catch fish, and they get tangled. Think connections and be curious as to where the connections will go.

Begin Now!, LLC

Begin Now!, LLC partners with people to co-facilitate maximum growth and development in intercultural, personal, and professional domains. Assessments, coaching, training, and facilitated travel available.

www.beginnowllc.com

Kelly Jahner-Byrne
Kelly Enterprises International

"Figure out how to keep yourself from feeling like you are crazy."

Kelly has three business silos that support each other as part of Kelly Enterprises International. As a managing director of a national network group for women entrepreneurs, CEO of a consumer goods direct selling organization, and nationally known speaker, Kelly knows how to leverage one business to support another. Her courage is to be admired as she has built her business by trying new opportunities and learning along the way.

Kelly's Advice ...

Research

When meeting new people be sure to research information about the individuals. You can learn so much online about a person's hot buttons and how to serve them. By focusing on others and how to serve them, you build valuable relationships to grow your business. Research yourself online, to see if the picture you present is the one you want.

Follow Up

If Kelly could give her younger self advice, she would tell herself to follow up! If you meet someone be sure to reach out to that new connection. The difference between success and failure can be how you follow up. We do too much "follow-on" or "following" and forget to reconnect in a meaningful way. A "like" on Facebook is not a follow-up, it is a follow-on. Following up makes it easy for people to stay connected to you. Your research about the person can help you when you follow up. You can mention a connection that is important to the other person to demonstrate that you're paying attention and adding value to the relationship. There is nothing more impressive than letting people know you took the time to learn more about them. LinkedIn and Facebook are great resources to research and learn about your new connection. Do something out of the ordinary to stay connected. It is too easy to be ordinary. Think of how to be extraordinary.

Investigate

Oftentimes, we are presented with an opportunity that may not seem to be a fit, but it is always worth investigating it further to understand more. It's paramount to understand the significance surrounding an event, a person, a business opportunity. Don't judge too quickly; know why you are saying yes or no to a person, a business opportunity, an event, etc. There may be great benefits or there may be nothing there, but you don't know unless you investigate.

Kelly Enterprises International

Kelly Enterprises International is a firm committed to sharing the HOW TO in business. Entrepreneurship is challenging and they can show you HOW to leverage for success. *Kelly Enterprises International* and Kelly Jahner-Byrne produce The HOW Conference, as well as business strategy events for entrepreneurs.

www.KellyJahnerByrne.com

Nancy Clairmont Carr
The Joy-Effect

"Everything I have done in all my career prepared me for this business."

Nancy's life path has taken her from the corporate world to her own business. As the owner of The Joy-Effect, Nancy is a transformational coach, bringing joy, abundance, and personal freedom to the lives of many. By paying attention to her own physical and emotional reactions to her corporate career, she chose to leave and follow her personal wellness path. Her decision to start her own business was made in a moment when she stated, "Today is the day I start my business."

Nancy is very clear about her ideal client and her programs to serve clients interested in change. This clarity has brought remarkable success in her short tenure of being in business.

Nancy's Advice ...

Being in alignment is the
most critical item in my work

Knowing how you can help others while maintaining your own health is an act of alignment. Begin by being "on purpose" with your work and being willing to speak and act on what you know and believe.

Set boundaries to make sure you are in alignment. "When I was in the corporate world," Nancy states, "I responded to the needs and goals of others. My health took a toll because of being out of alignment with myself. As I have moved to my own business, I recognize the importance of taking care of my health is just as important to my business as any other effort."

Everything you put in your body impacts you. The people you surround yourself with contribute to your experiences and beliefs that support you, your life, and your business. This critical body-mind-spirit-health awareness can create unlimited opportunities for success, but only if you are willing to pay attention to your personal alignment.

Create a support team inside and outside your business

Solopreneurship can be lonely and overwhelming. Having support from others is important so you can focus on your best work. Building a "team" can be accomplished via networking groups, virtual assistants, family, and coaches. You can't do it all; trying to do so will hold you back from growing and building. There are others who can do it better. Starting out, you may not know what or who you need. Once you get your hands into your business, ask yourself, "What am I *not* good at?" Then delegate or build a team.

Get up every day to learn more and serve more

Seek expertise from coaches, advisors, books, and seminars. Take what you learn and do it! Even if it is not right the first time, you can iterate until it fits for you. Fear of acting can be crippling. Accept that you may not do it perfectly, but you will learn as you go.

Learn to surrender to not knowing everything and listen to your internal guidance. We really know a lot more than we give ourselves credit for knowing! If we can get quiet with ourselves we can use our intuition. I am not responsible for the outcome. I am responsible for moving forward and serving. Let others determine their outcomes.

The Joy-Effect

Nancy Clairmont Carr is a coach, energy healer, speaker, and the founder of The Joy-Effect, a transformational coaching business. Nancy guides change-seekers to their desired lifestyles by removing success blocks in all areas and creating joy, abundance, freedom, and overall balance.

www.TheJoy-Effect.com

Charlotte Chipperfield

Chipperfield Media LLC

"I was able to merge my creative business talents with abilities."

Charlotte is the owner of Chipperfield Media, LLC, a marketing and social media consulting firm. She spent over a decade in the wine industry. As her journey in the wine industry expanded, she found herself focusing on the marketing aspects of this industry. Her love for analytics, creativity, and marketing led her to achieve her desire of owning her own business. She has been able to merge all of her strengths to create a business that works for her.

Charlotte's Advice ...

Ask for help

When you don't have a team, ask questions and reach out to your network to build your team. You need an accountant, a lawyer, and many others to support you. Your network is your greatest resource, but not if you don't use it. Continually be aware of the support you need and create clear goals to ask your network for possible connections. You might be surprised by the doors that open for you.

Get out of your own head

Get your mindset shifted so you can recognize when you are in your own way. Signs of this can be frustration, lack of efficiency, or being stuck. Stay out of the victim mode and move to the action mode. Failure can be the trigger to move you to victim mode. Take a step back and take a moment to think about shifts. Charlotte recognizes when she is "too much in her head" she becomes frustrated. It is a sign that she is pushing too hard and overanalyzing to the point of being stuck. Stepping back and taking a new look at the situation often removes the block and starts things moving forward again.

Be flexible

Flexibility can be a challenge. Hold yourself accountable, but know that things might change at a moment's notice and you will need to shift your priorities. It may lead you to new business services and creative ways to respond to your clients.

Charlotte shares the story of working with a client using services she had clearly defined. When the client asked her to provide a related, but new, version of this service, her first thought was, "No, that's not the plan." She decided to say "yes" and see what would happen. A new service emerged as a result, which has become a product she has provided to many other clients. She advises that being "planful" is appropriate as an entrepreneur, but cautions against shutting down opportunities. The balance between planful and flexible is critical for the entrepreneurial business.

Chipperfield Media

Chipperfield Media is a social media advisory firm that empowers companies to own their social media from the inside out and to build genuine connections with their customers through customized social media training, resources, and consulting.

She believes every company should own their social media because, when done correctly, social media is the best way to create authentic relationships with your customers to gain feedback, create community, and strengthen your bottom line.

www.chipperfieldmedia.com

Julie Danskin

Direct Selling Co.

"This one decision changed the direction of my family and my life!"

Julie has been in the top one percent of her Direct Selling Co. for the past thirty years. She capitalizes on her wisdom and knowledge by mentoring others and sharing her expertise.

Julie had a very successful non-profit executive career and decided one day that she wanted to oversee her own future. As she states, "I left my successful career to sell lipstick!" A friend introduced her to Mary Kay and it wasn't long before she jumped on board to try something different. May Kay's philosophies were in alignment with what Julie was looking for in her life. She started with a hope and a prayer and never looked back. This one decision impacted her and her family's life direction.

After all these years, Julie now passes along her wisdom through mentoring others. She enjoys supporting Millennials in growing their own successful businesses and finding the same kind of freedom that Julie created in her own life.

Julie's Advice ...

Nurture your inner voice

This is your inner wisdom. If you nurture this inner voice, it will guide you to take inspired action often, despite the noise of daily life and stakeholders' opinions. Many times, we settle for things and do not go for adventures we want and deserve. By nurturing your inner voice, you can begin to use your unique gifts and talents. What is your inner voice telling you? Thirty minutes of journaling every day can help you listen to that voice. Be intentional about what you listen to and who is in your life.

Vision

Vision conquers the feeling of being adrift at sea. It keeps you from getting in a rut. What if life could be different? How would you change things? Being intentional in your business requires you to have a sharp vision for your work and what you want to accomplish. Having a clear set of goals and desires attracts the right opportunities and clients to your business. Vision boards are one way to create the future you desire. Updating your vision board is necessary to keep your goals, passion, and direction alive. The vision board takes your goals a step beyond to get you the results and feelings you deserve.

Alignment

Entrepreneurial success comes from setting clear priorities and sticking to them. One of the largest challenges for the entrepreneur is the inability to wisely delegate. Say "no" to the trivial, put your energy where your talents are, and focus on income-producing activities. This also requires you to be very clear on what is in alignment and what is not. It takes courage to let go of what isn't in your best interest. Success as an entrepreneur is a total faith walk!

Independent Executive Senior Sales Director, Mary Kay

For over thirty years, Julie has mentored and coached thousands of women to create a lifestyle of liberty through successful at-home entrepreneurship. She has earned the use of many Pink Cadillacs and helps her customers perform a miracle before the mirror every day using Mary Kay products.

www.juliedanskin.com

Brenda DeMotte

Grief Demystified

"It's never done."

Brenda has had many doors and opportunities open from the people who crossed her path. From funeral director to social worker to author, speaker, and therapist, Brenda has allowed the course of her business and career to naturally emerge. Her newest book, *Grief Demystified*, is a powerful guide with real life stories and tools for gently moving through grief.

Brenda's inherent curiosity has helped her grow and expand her business. She has built a business that works for her, utilizes her talents, and creates a lifestyle that fits her family.

She built her book by writing newsletters with articles for her clients. Over time, she compiled the articles into the book, *Grief Demystified*. Her goal is to disseminate her tools for coping with grief to a wider group and expand her teaching.

Brenda's Advice ...

The most important piece is mentorship

Brenda "sucked up" every piece of information she could from the mentors in her life. It helped her build a life, construct a career, and get her where she wanted to go. She found her mentors by seeking out the brightest people around her and targeting the needs she had for her professional development. Her advice is to be intentional about what you are looking for, and allow the right mentors to show up. "You can have many mentors once you are clear about what you need."

Know yourself

There are many business formulas, but the pieces that are more elusive are the ones about you! "Who am I? What are my talents? Am I using these in the best way for me?" These questions came when she was most uncomfortable. Even though she was following what she thought was the "right" way, she was unhappy and questioning the process. It was this discomfort that led to her knowing more about herself and how she best operated as a business owner.

Learning about yourself is never done! As you and your business move forward, new discomforts will be created that force you to adapt and grow. When you feel you are "petting the cat the wrong way" it is time to evolve once again!

Balance is possible

There is no one prescribed way to do things. Brenda needed to define her style of work so she could find a business model that fit her. She wanted a life, not just a business. Once she defined what she wanted, she found it to be a continual fight to not feel guilty. All the "shoulds" became the messages to conquer. She found she had a successful business and lifestyle, but she fought to keep the balance. Once she honored her desire for balance, she began to attract more of the "right" clients. She did this by defining who she would work with and who was a bad fit.

It surprised her how well this balanced method worked and she refuses to return to her old way of doing business. Now, she answers three questions before she decides on new opportunities:

- Is it of value to me?
- Does it have meaning to me?
- Does it advance me to where I am going?

Professional Counseling & Grief Services, Inc. & Grief Demystified

Brenda DeMotte is a psychotherapist of thirty years who specializes in grief and the psychology of change. Her book, *Grief Demystified*, is a product of her years of working with and learning from those who have walked that path.

www.griefdemystified.com

Char Dobbs

Char Style and Image Management Consulting

"Trust that your business doesn't need to be exactly like someone else's."

Char Dobbs is an engineer turned image consultant. She combines her technical background and love for style to help professional women tell their story with authenticity and confidence. Char's connection with clothing started when she was young. She found herself working as an engineer, but was constantly pulled to her creative talents. After research and job shadowing, it became apparent that her long-held passion and talents aligned well with image consulting. It wasn't an easy transition, but with time and research, the business came together.

Char's Advice ...

It's okay to be different

You need to continually review where you are in your business and where you want to go. It is fine to have a different business model. Many will have advice for you, but you need to know what your business is and how it will work best for *you*. Coaching and role models can help build a foundation, but you need to set the course. You can get distracted by, "What did they do?" versus, "What can I create?" It can hold you back if you are always comparing yourself to others, and it is so easy to fall into that comparison model. On her business journey, Char sometimes questioned herself and her methods because others were not doing things the same way. At one point, when she was about to approach her business in an unconventional way, she decided to defer to her clients and ask for their input. They supported her idea and soon she developed new offers in her business.

Believe in yourself and your work

Cultivating confidence is a daily, hourly, second-by-second practice. One small thing can knock you off your rocker. That's why learning to have an unwavering belief in your work is critical. Even if you don't know the answer or the *how*, have confidence you will get there and trust yourself to find the answer. Being an active student of this lesson will help you build your business. It requires a different level of belief. You could be doing all the "right things," but there will always be people who will disagree with you. Push through because most of the time it is their "stuff," not yours!

Trust your gut

We've all heard this many times, but we are human and need to hear it repeatedly. Even if your ideas are crazy, trust yourself. The *why* and the *how* will be revealed. If you ignore your gut, it will come back to remind you of decisions you should have made. It sounds simple, but it is not easy.

Char Style and Image Management Consulting

Char Style and Image works to help women take control of how they show up in the world by supporting them in identifying personal styles that amplify their confidence and align with their personalities, careers, and lifestyle priorities. She is uniquely equipped to craft chic visual brands for ambitious professional women—a brand and wardrobe that tell their stories with authenticity and authority.

www.charstyleandimage.com

Julie Finch

Finch Law

"You can have a perfectly fabulous business and life."

Julie Finch has had a variety of law experiences. She has worked with business issues including trademarks, intellectual property, and transactional issues. When she was suddenly in a non-chosen transition, she decided to take on a few freelance projects. Julie says she "backed into" owning her business. She recognized that she wanted time to be with her daughter and decided to set up an office at home. Before she knew it, she loved having her own business and never returned to a corporate or firm position! Finch Law focuses on working with entrepreneurs to alleviate potential legal missteps such as trademark or contract issues.

She is now in a growth mode, which includes a business and marketing plan. She is also expanding her business by delegating some of the work to hired contractors. Her team is virtual and effectively allows Julie to do the work she is meant to do. In this way, she can build her client base without having employees.

Julie's Advice ...

Get comfortable with being uncomfortable

There is always something to learn, whether it be technical expertise or the daily challenges of running your business. Accept the fact that, as an entrepreneur, you will always encounter something in your day that will make you feel uncomfortable.

Several years ago, Julie took horseback riding lessons to support her daughter's desire to ride. Every time she had a lesson, she was fearful and certain she would NOT return alive. This became her basis for conquering her uncomfortable feelings in her business. She would ask herself, "Will this be worse than riding the horse?" The answer was always "no" and she would move forward.

Follow up, follow up, follow up

Consistent follow-up is critical. We are all busy people with many things to do. When others don't follow up or respond, you might take it personally.

You must get over that feeling as there are many reasons people don't respond. Continually follow up!

Don't let social media or email be your only contact points. It's easy to turn to social media and email, but personal connections make stronger connections.

Educate your market

You know what you do and you assume others also know. A common mistake made by entrepreneurs is talking, but not communicating. When we are small we tend to avoid talking about what makes us unique. We do this because it is so personal to us. When you are the figurehead, the business is *you*. Most of us, especially women, are not good about talking about ourselves or downplay our accomplishments. We forget how good we really are and how much we need to educate others about how good we are.

Owning a business is always a creative endeavor. As you grow and change, you need to continue to evolve and clarify your message in addition to educating your clientele.

Finch Law

Finch Law helps entrepreneurs build the right foundation for a profitable business. With an eye for alleviating marketing missteps (e.g. trademark infringement) and closing customer deals, Finch Law allows companies to confidently grow revenue and profits.

www.finch-law.com

Joan Gilles

Financial Planning Partners

"Perspective + experience + knowledge = resilience"

Joan Gilles has a long career in the financial services industry. She has a heart to serve her clients and finds her job energizing, rewarding, and just plain AWESOME! She made the move from working as a "girl Friday" to establishing herself in a role as a financial advisor with Financial Planning Partners.

Joan's Advice ...

Learn from your mistakes

Mistakes teach us resilience. When you fail, you are not defeated. You just need to pick yourself up and keep going. Your office needs to be a judgment free zone, both for yourself and your clients. Your goals may not change, but how you accomplish them can, based on what you learn. Just like the GPS in your car says "Recalculating" when you take a wrong turn, so can your goals recalculate when you make a mistake. Stop and recalculate.

You need to define what success means for you and not what it means for everyone else. A .400 batting average in baseball is a success, BUT that means the batter failed sixty percent of the time. What does success mean for you? How will you deal with failure?

Whatever you do, get fired up about it

Have passion around what you do. If you have passion, people will gravitate to you. Joan's dad said, "People don't care how much you know until they know how much you care." Lifehack.org defines passion as "an emotion to be acted upon... Fuel for the fire of action."[5] When we have passion for something, we love it even when we hate it.

Make choices to make money

If you pick something, be the best at it. It will fuel your passion as you learn and grow. There needs to be a balance between making money and finding your passion. It's a journey, not an epiphany.

Joan started in a support position in the financial arena and eventually found the passion to move forward in the financial field. She has met many entrepreneurs who are passionate about their business, but making no income. You *can* achieve both objectives if you consciously choose to balance your passion with your finances. For example, you may need to hold another job while you build your business. With time, this business may accommodate the income you desire and both needs will be met.

Focus on strengths and ignore weaknesses

Many people say build your weaknesses, but Joan says, "Ignore them. You won't be good at them anyway." When you focus on your strengths, you can be happier and less stressed. This leads to less failure and more passion. Capitalize on the gifts and blessings you have been given.

[5] Thompson, Braden. *What it means to have passion.* Lifehack. http://www.lifehack.org/articles/lifestyle/what-means-have-passion.html. Accessed 12/21/17.

Financial Planning Partners

Financial Planning Partners' mission is to provide financial management and consulting through the lens of customer values, intentions, and aspirations. They support savvy women in their financial journeys and believe finances don't have to be an obstacle.

www.financialplanpartners.com

Tera Girardin

Tera Photography LLC

"We, as women, keep ourselves small versus seeing the impact we make in the world."

Tera Girardin took her passion for photography and her personal experience with an autistic son to write her new book, *Faces of Autism*. She had the epiphany to write the book and could not turn back. She has now taken her successful photography practice to a new place by adding "author" to her title.

Tera's Advice ...

Float and flow

Stay in the flow where things are moving easily. Even though you are working hard, pushing for things to happen and creating stress for yourself will not assist you in serving your clients or building your business. "Floating" versus struggling is the key. It is not about the energy of the "hustling;" it is about the energy of "flow." Hustling is when you are frantically working to create outcomes that are not meant to be. Flow is when you allow things to happen based on the efforts you are making. Think of floating in the water. You need to relax and allow the float to happen. If you struggle, you won't be able to float. Struggling is the "hustle" mode. Relaxing is the float mode. It is not easy. Learn to recognize when you are in hustle mode and make a new decision to focus on the one thing you can do to move your businesses forward and stay in the flow.

Follow your own arrow

Have you ever heard "you should do it this way or you won't be successful?" YUCK! Stay out of your "shoulds" and the "shoulds" of others to build a business that works for you. When you go to trainings, you often hear messages on the way you "should" do things. Use these trainings to inform your unique business and not as a script you "should" follow.

Always honor how you work

One of the luxuries of being a small business owner is the freedom to create the schedule that works for you. When are you most productive? Honor it and create your schedule around those high-energy times. Don't force something that doesn't work or you will go back to struggling and ignoring the flow.

Take time to be creative with yourself

Sometimes we take something joyful and make it stressful. STOP IT! Make time to be creative with yourself by finding the fun and enjoyment in what you do, even if you can't monetize it. As a photographer, Tera finds time to take photos for pure enjoyment. If she has a photoshoot, she might add time to her schedule so she can photograph things just for fun. It is her way of continually reconnecting with her work and finding her joy.

Tera Photography

Tera is a natural light photographer in the Twin Cities, specializing in fresh, authentic portraits of children and their families. She has a special place in her heart for children with autism and her labor of love, *Faces of Autism* was published in April of 2017.

www.teraphotography.com

www.facesofautismbook.com

Louise Griffith

One Shining Light

"Honor your inner wisdom. If you don't, who will?"

Louise Griffith possesses a long history of supporting others in their growth and success. From elementary teacher to psychologist to success coach, she has now added internationally recognized speaker and author to her list of accomplishments. Louise is dedicated to inspiring and motivating individuals to build the best versions of themselves. Her latest book, *You Are Worth It*, delivers the tools to illuminate possibilities, inspire, create change, and transform lives. At seventy years old, Louise has learned many business lessons. Here are three she has found important in her journey...

Louise's Advice ...

Honor your inner wisdom

If you don't honor your inner wisdom, who will? Pausing to listen to your inner voice is an effective way to honor that wisdom and keep you from running to the chaos. Entrepreneurs can sometimes chase "shiny objects" and not intentionally choose the options that their inner wisdom selects. That insight provides grounded decisions.

Show up

Show up at events and meet people. It is about relationships. Building relationships will build your business. Be present at the events where you choose to network and increase your clientele, resulting in business growth.

Take one more step

Louise recently walked the Camino de Santiago in Spain. A key lesson from her Camino journey was "take one more step." Just as in her business, the next step keeps leading you to the destination. Whether the journey is hard or easy, the most important thing is to take the next step. Eventually, you will say, "I did it!" Along the way, allow yourself to receive love and support from others. There are many kind people who want to support you. Accept it!

One Shining Light

A masterful coach, Louise works with women who want to get past the past, discover what makes them tick, and unlock possibilities for what is next in their lives and work. She is the author of *You Are Worth It*.

www.oneshininglight.com

Irmadene Hanson

Magnify Your Influence

"No Negative Nellies"

Irmadene started her business after twenty-five years in a corporate position. Three years ago, she founded Magnify Your Influence, focusing on targeting the leaders in senior care who want to make a difference. This journey demonstrated her courage to find and follow her passion. Irmadene's work as a speaker and trainer, her personal wisdom, and her experience in senior care services has led to a business that honors her authentic self.

Irmadene's Advice ...

Do everything you can to be authentic

When Irmadene left the corporate world, she did many things to try and identify what was next. She took a few years to return to what she knows and loves. In that time, she has learned that people can sense if you are authentic. She advises: "If you do what you love and believe in, clients will come to you!" She also suggests to discover your authenticity by trying something new and reflecting on that experience for yourself. Pondering isn't enough for you to find authenticity. Rather, try something new and learn from it. If it is authentic, you will feel it in your heart and know it's what you are meant to do.

Spend dollars on the right things at the right time

Don't spend big money until you find your authenticity. This is a hard lesson and you sometimes only learn it once you've spent the money. Many people will tell you many ways to spend money. You will need to spend some dollars at first, but wait until you are clear before you spend dollars to advance your business.

Make sure you surround yourself with the right people

No Negative Nellies in your business life! You need people who pull you up. Additionally, if you are the smartest person in the room, you are in the wrong room. The right people will lead you to the right resources. They will support and celebrate your dreams. They will also challenge you to move forward and invest in what is right for you and your business.

Magnify Your Influence

An experienced speaker and trainer, Irmadene has guided many large and small groups toward transformation. Each presentation is created to highlight the key focus of the event or conference as it relates to leadership. Irmadene focuses on growing the audience's concepts of connection, influence, communication, and personal growth.

www.irmadene.com

Connie Hertz

Living in the Glow

"If we key into our 'self,' we all have amazing intuition."

Dream coach, motivational speaker, author, and entrepreneur, Connie Hertz teaches people the art of finding lasting joy and prosperity, no matter what they have been through.

Connie began her career as an oncology nurse. Growing up, she knew she wanted to be a nurse, as she cared deeply about helping others. Along the way, she has taken many personal growth courses. Her number one value is to live life to help others. Through challenging life changes, she was guided toward other personal growth opportunities. These courses led her to use her life story as a stepping stone to move her forward and create a new joy in her life. She became certified as a Dream Coach, determined to provide the same opportunities for joy to others.

Connie's Advice ...

Hire coaches—not just one

You need different coaches for unique needs: health and nutrition, business, and spiritual. If you are not great with discipline and consistency, let others help you grow that muscle as well. Coaches are an investment in yourself and your mission. Connie has hired various coaches over the course of her business and has found that each coach has contributed to her success by bringing various perspectives.

Discipline and consistency

Sometimes business is not easy...and neither is being disciplined. You can be smart, but it can also be challenging to stay consistently motivated. Discipline and consistency are integral to grow your business. You want habits that cultivate growth in your business. As an example, Connie is disciplined to consistently attend key networking groups and to promote her business through social media. Both have resulted in expanding the awareness and growth of her business.

Learn to take risks

Even if you are afraid, it is important to take a few risks to move your life forward. Think about what you would do if there were no obstacles in your way. What would the dream look like? Allow yourself to see the possibilities. You never know how doors may open to make the dream a reality. Even though dreaming can feel like a risk, allow yourself to dream.

Never quit

There are going to be days when you are discouraged. As you try new things, you will be stretched personally. Some things will go well, and others won't. All experiences allow you to build and grow. Your messages and what you learn are so important. Use each step as an opportunity to grow. Have patience with yourself and your learning curve.

Living In The Glow

Connie gives women a blueprint to achieve their dreams and goals. She practices both one-on-one and group coaching.

www.conniehertz.com

Kathryn Hoy

UBS Financial Services

"Sharing is the new selling."

Kathryn has over thirty-seven years of experience building a financial advising practice. As a female in the financial industry, Kathryn is dedicated to the mission of ensuring people are ready when the unexpected happens in life.

Over the years, she has had many roles in the financial world and transitioned to her own practice five years ago. She loves asking the questions and digging into "why" someone needs to care about their financial picture. Her unique focus on preparing for the unexpected creates a value for others. She learned this from her mother, who taught her to be prepared for the unexpected. This preparation led to a more "planful" outcome when her mother became ill and passed away.

Kathryn's Advice ...

Selling is not a terrible thing

As a young girl, Kathryn would make her dad sell her Girl Scout cookies because she thought selling was bad. She felt she was pushing people. Since that time, she has recognized that what she is selling is what people need. If they don't want it, they can say "no." If you have a great idea, share it with people. You are obligated to share your services, but customers get to decide if they want to buy. Sharing is the new selling.

Have regular, disciplined communication with your clients

Your clients want regular contact, especially if you have a service-oriented business. A communication plan is important to know your clients. When you call and check in, you continue to create value to inform your client base. Regular conversations help clients stay informed. This disciplined communication makes relationships stronger and ultimately brings more business.

You can't do everything on the internet

Be careful of thinking you can do everything on the internet. Yes, you can gain knowledge through Google, but who can you bounce ideas off of online? Who will hold your hand or provide input if you only use the internet? If you want to spend time searching and becoming the expert, do it. However, relationships and trusted advisors are important in making the journey easier.

UBS Financial Services

As a thirty-seven-year veteran of financial services, Kathryn helps people feel at ease, not defensive with where they are financially. She believes people want to be heard, not sold, and want to work with a competent, caring, and responsive financial advisor.

www.financialservicesInc.UBS.com

Kristi Hughes

The Fermented Experience

"Everything is figure-out-able."

Kristi started her career as a paramedic. After a career-ending injury, she needed to search for something new. She was working part-time in a retail wine business when she decided to explore the wholesale side of selling wine. In the process, she discovered the market demand for wine travel experiences. Her own passion for travel, wine, and hospitality led to her founding The Fermented Experience. Kristi provides wine country experiences several times during the year to locations throughout the world.

Kristi's Advice ...

Devote time to personal development every day

Giving time to yourself each morning sets the stage to approach the day. Don't let the negative bird chirp in your ear. Set your tone. Everything is figure-out-able. Kristi spends time every day reading or listening to personal or business development books or audios. She finds this provides her the necessary mindset to solve whatever comes her way during the day.

Don't wait to ask for capital

If you wait to ask for money until you need it, your bank may not be willing to give it to you. The criteria for business loans change. Sometimes, the banking world is supportive of small business and sometimes the criteria is so high it is impossible to obtain a loan. Providing a business strategy that is clean and proactive will allow you to be ready with capital when the time arrives.

Build relationships versus a website

Getting to know people in-person is more important than your internet presence. Talking to others and finding your audience is essential. Relationships can also lead to partnering with other businesses to enhance both of your business successes. Finding your tribe of positive supporters will build your foundation. Kristi found one of her strategic partners through relationships she formed while employed at a wine shop. She has found other connections at networking events. Her efforts to build relationships has resulted in greater business success than any technology efforts she has tried.

The Fermented Experience

The Fermented Experience creates priceless memories and quality time while connecting hearts amid wine country all around the world. Kristi does this by putting together all-inclusive travel packages. Kristi Hughes, Certified Wine Professional, is a personal guide on these promised world-class, bucket list wine country experiences. The Fermented Experience also offers wine, beer, and spirits seminars throughout the year, as well as wine consulting.

www.thefermentedexperience.com

Carol Kaemmerer

LinkedIn for Savvy Executives

"Who knew that adversity could lead to so much fun!"

Carol provides training and consulting to executives on LinkedIn. Her latest book, *LinkedIn for Savvy Executives*, is the first book focused on using LinkedIn to effectively power executive-level careers.

Carol has owned her own marketing consulting firm since 1986. She worked exclusively with one large corporate client for twenty years. That came to an end when the client chose to redirect marketing services to New York. This put her out of business! What would she do next? Despite feeling like a personal rejection, she began to discover the power of LinkedIn and how few people were using this tool effectively. As she debated her next steps, she was busy helping her friends build their LinkedIn profiles. They were so pleased, they began referring others. It became clear that this was her next business niche.

Carol's Advice ...

I don't have to be someone else's spokesperson to have a voice

Carol recognizes that she is a subject matter expert and has a product/ service of value and not a "pass-through tool." When she acknowledged that she was making a difference in the lives of others, she began to own her talent and business expertise. She also recognized the unique perspective she brings. The feedback from others clarified her efforts. This also led to writing her book.

Have a well-defined niche

When you provide one-on-one coaching, you really need to like the person or you will be miserable. Carol knows with whom she works best. These clients are willing to pay for her services, value her input, and refer other similar clients her way.

Take care of yourself
so you can be your best

Every day, Carol fuels herself so she can serve others. Exercise is an essential component for her. She also knows she needs social interaction to fuel her soul. Solopreneurs can be lonely and lose energy. Carol knows that including social interactions in the day will help keep her energy strong. She also values aesthetic care as a component of her self-care. For Carol, that means having her hair and nails done on a regular basis to help her feel confident and more comfortable with her clients.

CarolKaemmerer.com

Carol Kaemmerer is a professional speaker, personal branding coach, and author of *LinkedIn for the Savvy Executive: Promote Your Brand with Authenticity, Tact and Power*. Carol is passionate about helping businesses and executives leverage the power of LinkedIn to increase their visibility and influence, engage with their ideal audiences, and cultivate reputations as thought leaders.

www.carolkaemmerer.com

Nicole Keirnes

Keirnes Law

"I wanted to do things my way!"

Entrepreneur plus lawyer, Nikki is the founding partner of Kiernes Law. Starting her firm right out of law school, she focuses on family law and alternative dispute resolution strategies. She knew from her second year of law school that her ambition was to form a new type of law practice and her training in mediation influenced her business model. Even though she was not sure about this new endeavor, she took a leap of faith and moved ahead. Kiernes Law has recently joined forces with Bernstein Private Wealth Management.

Nikki's Advice ...

Know your strengths

It's important to recognize and respect individual strengths. Working against one's own strengths is an uphill battle. Using individual uniqueness can make the difference. Nikki believes that using your strengths can build success. While she did not know many lawyers who set up their own practice right out of law school, she did know and follow her own strengths. Nikki used assessments and discovered her natural entrepreneurship tendencies. These strengths and unique ideas about an innovative approach to law practice led to building a business that works for her and attracts the right clients.

Be flexible with plans

Opportunity is always around; the challenge is recognizing it. In overthinking things, people miss the proverbial boat, so it's important to pay attention. By paying attention, new networking opportunities and clientele will present themselves. As the network grows, clients will begin to come from random locations. It is that growth and randomness that requires you to remain flexible and continue to share your business.

Lead with emotion

Don't be afraid to show emotion. Most people think lawyers are unemotional. Deeper relationships grow when a person connects with another person on an emotional level. Clients build trust, become friends, and refer others because of the care shown.

Business owners are amazingly resilient

As a business grows, there are new opportunities and challenges. The issues facing a startup business will be different five years down the road. There will always be new challenges. The focus is to appreciate one's own resilience and ability to figure things out. Owning a business is not predictable, so it's essential to be willing to tackle the new. There will be a mix of joy and challenge.

Keirnes Law, PLLC
(Now merged with Bernstein
Private Wealth Management)

Nikki has now transitioned her business to Bernstein Private Wealth Management. Nikki is responsible for providing investment and wealth planning advice to individuals and families and their trusts, estates, foundations, endowments, and pension plans. In conjunction with Bernstein Private Wealth Private Management, Nikki provides counsel to clients and their professional advisors on a variety of matters, including tax and estate planning, multigenerational asset allocation, individual and corporate retirement planning, and the sale of closely held businesses.

www.bernstein.com

Denise Krogman

Pillow Talk and Comforters

"None of our paths are straight."

Denise Krogman is a woman of wisdom who writes from her soul. She is an author by heart and a realtor by profession. Her latest book, *Pillow Talks and Comforters*, came from her own lessons and personal journey. Her divorce left her needing to determine how she would proceed with her life and financial resources. She worked full-time, raising children and starting her profession as a realtor.

While these were the most challenging times for her, they also built the foundation for what she is doing today. Writing has always been a source of peace and support for Denise. Her book provides a vehicle to deliver her message of support to others.

Denise's Advice ...

Listen and learn from those around you

It is critical to surround yourself with people who are positive, supportive, and listen to what you must say. Everyone is so busy talking that we often forget to listen. Connecting with others who have different perspectives can teach you innovative ways to think and grow. The exchange of listening and supporting will help grow and build yourself and your business.

Diversify your opportunities to grow and change

Denise is not the same woman as several years ago, and neither is anyone else. However, each person is still the same "child" with our gifts and talents unique to the world. That child can grow and change by experiencing new opportunities. When Denise started her book, the purpose and direction changed. Feedback from others and the writing experience led her to new discoveries. The flexibility to diversify her experiences led to an even greater purpose.

Don't wait for approval to take risks

Denise spent most of her life as a rule follower. Over time, she has learned to take risks. "You can fall down and you can fail, but if you do, simply pick yourself up and start again." Fear only has power if a person gives it power. Enjoy the ride by making use of time and purpose in life. The biggest gifts in Denise's life have been the people who didn't believe in her. They taught her to be compassionate towards others and toward herself.

Author of PILLOW TALKS AND COMFORTERS:
Inspirations, Reflections, and Ponderings

What secrets does your pillow know about you? In her vulnerable sharing of real life moments, this book will leave you wondering if Denise has been reading your mind! This is a collection of true stories about real people and life-changing moments. Whether light-hearted laughter or deep soul searching, your own *Pillow Talks and Comforters* moments will forever be changed.

www.denisekrogman.com

Sarah Leitschuh

Marriage and Family Therapy

"When I could come around to accept my process and reasons why I am building my business, I became more confident and knew that I was putting the right energy into the world."

Sarah Leitschuh has her own practice as a marriage and family therapist. She has built her practice to balance her family and work goals. Her goals changed when she became a mom. She has intentionally built her time and commitment to her business as her children grow. She not only sees therapy clients, but works to support other therapists to grow the practice that balances their life and business goals.

Sarah's Advice ...

Accept your own process and avoid comparing yourself to others

There are times when you think, "I should," or compare yourself to others when they are on a different journey. Accepting yourself and where your business needs to be brings the right clients and business growth. Growth is not the only goal that matters as you build a model that fits for you. "Comparison is the thief of joy," says Theodore Roosevelt. Letting go of comparison can build the confidence you need to successfully create a business that works for you.

Know what makes you unique in your business

In the early years, Sarah was a passive business owner and followed the traditional practice-building model (e.g. website, ads). Over time, she realized she needed to have a way to stand out from the crowd of therapists from which clients could choose. Once she determined her ideal client and how she needed to speak to that person, she attracted the right kind of customer to tap into her unique tools and perspectives. She adopted an educational and approachable process that serves the ideal client with healthy tools which are unique to her and her practice.

Focus on relationships

Reach out to groups and professionals who also serve your ideal clients. The internet can be a magical source of information to find the possible resources available. For Sarah, community education and moms' groups were ideal connections. Through internet searches, she found prospects who could benefit from the educational tools she created and reached out to them. The worst thing that can happen is that people don't want to talk to you. You simply move on to the next contact.

Adopt an attitude of abundance

When you first start a business, it can be scary. You often feel that everyone should be your client. However, that is not realistic. Some clients will be great for you. Some will be better for others. With an attitude of abundance, you can refer clients to others, knowing the right clients will show up for you. Being a resource serves you, clients, and referral sources.

Sarah Leitschuh Consulting, PLLC

Sarah Leitschuh is a Licensed Marriage and Family Therapist who practices in Eagan, Minnesota. In addition to providing therapy services for families, Sarah also provides supervision, training, and coaching for other mental health professionals.

www.sarahleitschuhcounseling.com

Michelle Mazzara

Luvafoodie

"I love the creative aspects of my work the most."

Michelle Mazzara found she was missing something in her life when it came to seeking a relationship. She was tired of traditional dating sites. She wanted relationships that shared similar interests, particularly, an interest in food. She decided to create a relationship business where "foodies" of all ages could connect with others to share reviews, recipes, and interest in food.

This concept evolved into a community of foodies, not a focus on dating. She also develops and sells high quality food products available for sale in grocery stores and on her website.

Michelle's Advice ...

Keep your goals attainable and realistic

So many people, as they start a business, go to the very extreme of what the business could be. The reality is that you build over time. Setting attainable monthly and six-month goals keeps the business in motion and leads to adapting as you learn. Realistic checklists will help build your success. Lofty and unattainable goals will only lead to feelings of defeat. Every night before you stop working, look at what you accomplished that day and plan for the next. It is daily actions that will lead to growth.

Time management is essential to success

Each individual needs to determine the best way to manage their time. Wasting time doing nothing or day dreaming will slow the growth of your business. If you are NOT good at time management, find a process or tools to assist you. Discipline is a key ingredient to be a successful entrepreneur. This discipline leads to action. Action leads to business growth and results.

Business plans are not set in stone

As you build and grow, you will edit and develop your business plan. Learning and experiences provide additional information that informs what your clients will buy and expands your business opportunities. A willingness to listen and observe is crucial for entrepreneurs. The mission (the core), may not change, but the products and services may. In other words, the "why" does not change, but the "how" will expand and grow.

Luvafoodie

Luvafoodie is a gourmet consumable brand that connects all people together who share a passion for food and beverage.

www.luvafoodie.com

Patty McLain

Summit Mortgage

"You can't be the jack of all trades. You need professionals to move your business forward."

Patty McLain is a Residential Loan Officer. She has been helping people finance homes since 1991, after she was introduced to the mortgage business by a realtor friend. When she was first starting out in the business, she was originally told she would not be able to do the job. Her fire and determination were ignited and she set out to prove she could succeed. Soon, she became a continual high performer. She has now started her own home buyer education site to share her wisdom and untangle the complex mortgage process.

Patty's Advice ...

Hire professionals

We often try to save money and do it ourselves. Patty has learned how much she didn't know when she began to hire professionals. The result is a much more professional website and brand.

Be yourself; be authentic

Being in the business twenty-four years, Patty has attended numerous workshops on how to build her business. While the information was always useful, she found that clients were more attracted to her when she used the information to expand her authenticity versus becoming the "new model" of someone else's work.

She learned that being yourself allows you to attract the people you were meant to serve. You can't serve everyone, but you can serve the ideal clients that fit *you*. The lightbulb went on and she felt, "Thank goodness! I can be myself and have a stronger business!"

Align yourself with a company
that shares your values

As a loan officer, Patty needed to build and grow her business. However, relating to the right parent company was critical for providing a foundation for her business. Once she connected to a company that shared her values, she could provide her clients the type of service and commitment she believed in.

Summit Mortgage Corporation

Patty McLain has been helping clients finance homes since 1991 and has become known as an expert in the mortgage industry. She has gained respect in the real estate community by always doing the right thing and going the extra mile to make sure everything goes smoothly.

www.homebuyereducationonline.com

Brenda Sterling Meyers

Sterling Teas

"Since I didn't have a roadmap, I was making it up as I went along."

Brenda Sterling Meyers is the creator and president of Sterling Teas, based in Rockwell, Texas. Sterling Teas is celebrating eleven years as a leading Texas-based importer and artisan blender of premium loose-leaf teas and herbal blends. When Brenda started her business, she had no real plan; she was making tea blends for fun. During an event, she put out her teas for people to try. She had such a strong interest that she left the event knowing there was a business to be built. This led to her opening a small tea shop. Eventually, she started selling to restaurants. This expanded her business to wholesale. Today, her business includes ninety wholesale stores. She just completed the Goldman Sacks 1000 and is very clear on her plan and direction.

Brenda's Advice ...

Don't kick yourself for making wrong decisions

In 2009, Brenda was asked to add direct selling to her business plan. She moved in this direction, which resulted in quick growth. However, it was a model that did not work well for Brenda. She was miserable and found she lacked financial backing to truly grow this business. It also took her away from her retail and wholesale business. When she made the decision to close the direct selling side of the business, it upset many people. It was a hard decision for Brenda and it impacted her for over a year. Something inside said, "Focus and get back in it." When she did, the wholesale side of her business grew. She sees this decision as a learning experience and a necessary stepping stone.

Go with your gut when dealing with people

When you have a good thing going, people want to work with you. They have the best intentions, but it might not always be in your best interest. Many people have approached Brenda and she has taken on strategic connections, only to find the other person does not follow through. Brenda's suggestion is to always listen to those individuals, but do what you think is right for you. Don't respond to everything everyone wants you to do. Be kind, but clear on your brand and direction. Follow the core of what you want in your business.

Don't be afraid to say "yes" to something you are not sure you can do

Brenda is someone who always wants all the ducks lined up before she acts. Over the years, she has found she can do a lot more than she thought she could do. There were many things she could have said "no" to, but it would have stopped the growth of her business. The "yes" can be difficult if there is uncertainty. Brenda believes if you own your business, you are already able to push yourself. Push yourself a little more. Don't be afraid. Talking with others and having mentors can assist you in having the courage to move forward.

Sterling Tea

Sterling Tea is a leading Texas-based importer and artisan blender of premium loose-leaf teas. They source the finest natural ingredients and craft their teas in small batches to provide superior taste and aroma. Every cup is infused with love!

www.sterlingtea.com

Cindy Moy

Hot Flash Sisters

"Things change as you build your business."

Cindy Moy is the founder and CEO of Hot Flash Sisters, a free health and social app for women in perimenopause. The app lets women track their symptoms, get beyond feelings of isolation, and get more out of doctor visits. The app had over 1,000 downloads within the first ten weeks after launch.

Cindy transitioned from her work as an attorney when she realized a gap in the marketplace for women in perimenopause. Her research and personal experience led to a mission she could not ignore. She has now created a community of women.

Cindy's Advice ...

You don't need to have all the answers before you begin

It is important to recognize that things will change as you build your business. You do need to have the time and energy to address new things as they arise. If you are in the tech market, a six-month or five-year plan will not serve you because things change so quickly. Know where you are going and include the time to evaluate and adjust.

Build a network and relationships

Everyone you know is in your network. Networking is about building relationships, not just a sale. Some people think there are only certain people with whom they should network—MISTAKE! Any person is a person worth knowing. You never know who they know. Asking for help in your network will open doors you didn't even know were available to you.

You can't do it all

You can't build a business, run a home, raise your children, manage life, and do it perfectly. Let go of perfectionism. Feel guilty if you must, but keep going. Your child will survive if they have to make their own sandwich for dinner.

There will always be more lessons

When you run a business, something new is thrown at you every day. Cindy's business has pivoted in many directions in the last ten weeks. Even though she is not used to adapting so quickly, she allowed herself to learn the lessons and adjust. Cindy started Hot Flash Sisters with an idea of what was needed, but had no clue how to create an app. She also didn't know all the factors to consider for the perimenopausal woman. As she moved forward, her attitude of learning, solving the immediate next step, and enrolling the support of advisors allowed the success of her app to grow beyond her expectations.

Vorsdatter Limited

Hot Flash Sisters is a mobile platform for women to track perimenopause symptoms and talk to other women in same phase of life.

www.hotflashsisters.com

Paula Norbom

Talencio

"Be proactive and make sales happen."

Paula Norbom gets her energy by helping others succeed. As she was building her executive career in health technologies, she succeeded through the power of connections and collaboration. She finds joy in facing challenges head-on and energizing her team to get to the right answers quickly.

Talencio is a staffing firm focusing on technology for the health industry. Talencio was created because Paula loves the energy, excitement, integrity, and compassion found in health technology. She also enjoys working with the very bright people the industry attracts. Talencio was born while Paula held a side job and built the foundation of her business.

Paula's Advice ...

Recognize your DNA

When you operate from your strengths, the fear of moving forward diminishes. Paula has found StrengthsFinder to be a beneficial tool for understanding herself and her team. We all migrate to our comfort zones, but the sooner you understand your strengths, the more effective you can become.

Selling must be a primary activity

Sitting and waiting for referrals is a scary place to be. You need to be proactive and make sales happen. Paula was fearful of sales and marketing, but knew she needed to grow this area as a critical element of her business.

She spent time learning how to improve her sales abilities. Classes, podcasts, books, and mentors have all increased her selling skills. She has also hired experts to expand her social media presence. She devotes time to knowing what is happening in the industry so she can continually connect with her clients and prospective clients.

Starting and sustaining a business is incredibly hard

Stamina and arduous work is important to grow your business. There are many events that you can't predict or control with your clients, the economy, or the world at large. You need to plan for a variety of outcomes to continue your business. There will always be "costs" to you as a business owner. Calculate the costs in time, money, and family to see if it is worth it to dedicate yourself to your business. The dedication is important to sustain your business over time.

Understand the DNA of your team

At some point in your growth, you will need to have a team of people to support you. Whether this team is virtual, contracted, or employees, understanding who is on your team and the talents they bring is important.

Leveraging the strengths of each team member creates an internal environment of trust and generates better outcomes for clients. Spending time and creating a dialogue to understand the team is important for your business.

Talencio, LLC

Talencio is a top specialized recruiting agency and staffing firm that provides vetted and accomplished professionals to the health technology community.

www.talencio.com

Cecelia Otto

An American Songline

"You can shoot for the moon, but aim for the rocket ship first."

Cecelia Otto (aka "Cece") is a classically trained singer, composer, and author who founded An American Songline. She brings her love of history and music together by performing across the United States at historical sites.

In 2015, she published a book to commemorate the World War I show that she created and performed across the United States. She also financed her book *The Ten Commandments of Crowd Funding* through Kickstarter and now provides information to help others do the same.

Cece's Advice ...

When the road less traveled doesn't work, create your own path

We need to rise above white noise to create a niche. Even if you have a niche, you might still be following a path that others have used. By creating your own path, it can keep the passion alive, despite the fear. Planning is important as you create your own path. You can shoot for the moon, but aim for the rocket ship first. As you start to move on the path, the rest of the path will appear right in front of you.

Build and maintain a community

When you build your own path, you need to remember there are people standing along the shoulder of your road to cheer you on. Stay loyal to those who have helped you in the past. Make it part of your business practice to nurture and stay devoted to the people in your community. They will support you as you move along your journey.

Embrace grace within chaos

There will be moments of chaos and uncertainty. Step back during those times and think about what is going right. Focus on the things going well to strengthen your resolve. Cece tells the story of arriving at a performance only to find the setup was not as she expected. She could have easily become distracted by the problems but, instead, stayed focused on what was going right. She calls this "handling things with grace." The result was a successful performance with a delighted audience.

An American Songline

Created by singer and composer Cecelia "Cece" Otto, An American Songline® is an ongoing project dedicated to preserving and sharing the story of America through unique, experiential musical performances. American Songline performances entertain, educate, and delight thanks to Cece's unique ability to engage modern audiences with the songs and stories of a simpler time.

www.americansongline.com

Cathy Paper

RockPaperStar

"The worst they can say is 'no.'"

RockPaperStar has been in business for ten years. The focus is coaching and marketing for select authors and unique speakers. Cathy has previously founded and launched three companies: Paper Plus Recycling, Live Dynamite, and Jump Start Results. She has also helped launch several New York Times Best Sellers. Cathy has combined her interest in marketing with her interest in leadership and coaching to form RockPaperStar.

She didn't start small. She was hired by Harvey McKay and assisted him with online marketing and product development. After one year, she convinced Harvey to be her first client. From there, she created her own model which became RockPaperStar. Cathy thinks big and leads her clients to do so as well.

Cathy's Advice ...

Take care of yourself

Celebrate your wins. You are the business owner and wear many hats. Celebrating wins is a way to acknowledge the work complexity and results you achieve. The sooner you learn to care for yourself and illuminate your wins, the easier you will find your life as an entrepreneur. If you are going to be a stable leader and advisor for others, you need to weave through the chaos and find the wins for you and your business. Cathy also recommends that you take breaks for exercise and disconnect from technology. Find your tools to be disciplined and care for yourself. Cathy uses "no technology Tuesdays" as a way to focus and care for herself.

Ask others for advice and build good relationships

There are others who have done this before you. Ask others for advice and learn from them. These relationships provide you a foundation of support to move you in the direction that works for you. It's okay to say, "I don't know" or admit to others you might not be succeeding. Seek the advice to solve your dilemma and then move on. Every step adds to the clarity of your direction. It also strengthens the support team you build. Some people will not fit in your support team. Be okay with letting them go and moving on to others. You are the leader of your business even when you are uncertain of the direction.

Ask for the order and follow the metrics

Pay attention to the numbers. How many proposals do you write? Are you pursuing referral sources? Do you ask for the order? The metrics can tell you what is working and what is not. It can help you see when you are off-track in your marketing and sales efforts. Cathy finds referral sources are a strong source of business revenue. By tracking her referral sources and sending thank you notes to these sources, the metrics show this continues to foster continued referrals. Metrics can provide the clarity and focus for where to spend your time.

RockPaperStar Inc.

RockPaperStar and its team specializes in accelerating business owners into motion through power networking, coaching, promotional marketing, and creative development. The company provides strategic guidance for select motivated individuals to reach their desired results and monetize their message through PR, books, speaking, and training...No matter where you are in the process.

www.rockpaperstar.com

Tara Peyerl

Salesforce.com

"What do you do when what you do becomes more important than who you are?"

What do you do when you decide you no longer want to run your own business and want to return to the corporate world? When Tara Peyerl left her corporate position to start The Light Compass, she knew she enjoyed coaching others for success in their life and work. She also tended to attract others who asked for her guidance. These were great signs that starting her own coaching business made sense. It also allowed Tara the opportunity to regain something she was losing in the corporate world. *What* she was doing became more important than *who* she was.

Tara enjoyed working with clients, but missed working alongside a team. By leaving the corporate world, it became clear that she liked the dynamics of working in an organization. She also discovered she could bring her coaching strengths to that world if she were with the right organization. After careful introspection, Tara decided it was best for her and her talents to return to a corporate position. Tara began a search for that organization and is now working with SalesForce.com

Tara's Advice ...

Run your own race

You can only be aware of who *you* are and what fits for *you*. Even if the experts say, "This is the way to do it," you need to be in alignment with yourself and build a business that works for you. Listen to your own voice and take time to listen. Insights will come and the next steps for you and your business will become apparent. In Tara's case, the insights into her personal preferences led her back to a corporate position. She describes her concerns that others would think she failed in her business. What she recognized is that the opinions of others were less important than following her own path.

There will always be mountains to climb

There is always the "once this happens, all will be great" message. Life is meant to give you new challenges and questions. New mountains are new opportunities and you will find the answers. Believe in yourself and check your beliefs along the way. Are they *your* beliefs or are they the beliefs of others?

Tara's journey to entrepreneurship added to her understanding of herself and that her needs were better served in the corporate environment. One of her lessons in being an entrepreneur was the value of business development and sales. Rather than this being the reason she left her business, it became a skillset she harvested and will use in her new role at SalesForce.com.

Setbacks aren't fatal

If you strive for the goal and don't hit it, it doesn't mean the goal is wrong. It might mean you need to explore new paths. Being called to something greater means you need to build new muscle. Tara's business allowed her to rekindle who she is and not be defined by her title. As a result, Tara was able to rejoin the corporate world with a new perspective. The path was not wrong; it guided her to a new, more significant path.

Salesforce.com

Tara is a Customer Success Director for retail at Salesforce. She accelerates customer return on investment by making sure the products they have purchased are being optimized.

www.salesforce.com

Amy Quale

Wise Ink

"I learned early on that books can change the world."

Amy Quale has a passion for English, but what does an English major do for a career? As co-founder of Wise Ink Publishing, Amy decided to combine her entrepreneurial passion with her English expertise. Wise Ink started as a blog to educate authors and, when Amy and her co-founder were at a crossroads, they decided to start their own company. They developed an individualized model to allow each author to get exactly what they need to publish their book. Today, Wise Ink Publishing works with self-motivated authors to publish books that matter.

Amy's Advice ...

Have goals that are giving *and* selfish

Create two-tiered goals. One tier is what you want to achieve for others. The other tier is what you want to achieve for yourself. This creates the drive to keep going. Amy also gives this advice to her authors. She acknowledges that we are human beings and need to both give value and receive value. The two-tiered goals create the motivational connection.

Focus on your right client

It's hard to stay focused and grow if you don't know who your right client is. You can't build your mission and direction, or attract the right clients, if you don't have clarity in this area. When this is clear, your business will grow and you will know where to market. Taking on clients who don't fit, but bring revenue, will distract you and limit your ability to take on the "right" client.

Manage through effectively delegating

Know the importance of your time and the importance of delegating. You must be honest about what you can and cannot do, both for your personal stress level and the growth of your business. It's easy to get caught in short-term urgent tasks and not schedule time to address the long-term strategic needs of your business. If you don't find people you trust that you can delegate to, you won't delegate. Spending time on building your team will be worth the long-term success of your business.

Wise Ink Creative Publishing

Wise Ink is a publishing agency that helps independent authors publish books that matter. They provide a holistic approach to the publishing process.

www.wiseinkpub.com

Gwen Reidl

GROW Coaching and Consulting

"I can't say I was completely committed when I first started."

After fifteen years as an internal consultant, Gwen decided to make a leap and start her own business. Passionate about helping leaders grow their skills and improve communication, she founded her own coaching and consulting business, GROW Coaching and Consulting. Her entrepreneurial journey has proven to be a learning and growing experience for her.

Gwen's Advice ...

Be prepared, as you might be surprised where your business comes from

Shortly after Gwen started her business, a coffee meeting led to a project with a Fortune 500 Company. Her openness and courage to connect with others has led to business she did not think was possible. Much of her work has come from people she has known for a long time, but she didn't predicted she would get work from these connections. On the other hand, the groups she expected to get work from have not always followed through.

Be open, but focused and intentional

As an internal consultant, Gwen had a wide array of responsibilities. In her own business, she finds that she is best focused when projects align with herself and her talents. Because of that, she has learned to say "yes" to the right client. While Gwen is open to discussion on projects, she is clear on the talents and projects that are the best fit for her. Taking on projects that are not a good fit often come back to haunt her.

It takes time

It takes time to figure out what you want, your value to the business, and to build relationships. Potential clients will help define and narrow the focus of what you want to do and what you will sell. You can love a certain process or product, but if it doesn't sell, you don't have a business. Allow yourself the time to reflect, learn, and make decisions about your business.

GROW Coaching and Consulting, LLC

GROW Coaching and Consulting, LLC provides one-on-one coaching and customized leadership development programs to technical professionals so they can bring their best selves to work each day. They focus on building self-awareness and strengthening interpersonal skills so that teams can better communicate, cooperate, and collaborate.

www.growcoachingconsulting.com

Margaret Smith

UXL

"There were times when I felt like an imposter."

Margaret Smith is a career and leadership coach, speaker, and author. Margaret founded UXL after her own transition and discovered that she was passionate about contributing to others, based on her own experience and clarity. Her latest book, *The Ten-Minute Leadership Challenge*, highlights her wisdom and lessons learned from thirty years of leadership. She now coaches, trains, and mentors others to achieve success in their work and life.

Margaret's Advice ...

Don't think you need to create everything today, by yourself

Building a business takes time. Being an entrepreneur requires managing many things. As you build your business, recognize and accept that it will take time. There is no way it can be created in one day, AND don't assume you should do it alone. People are willing to help if you are clear on what you need at any moment in time. Always keep a list of three things you need so you are ready when people ask how they can help. Also, be willing to give to others. When you give, something will come back to you.

Get out there and try it

You must narrow your scope and get focused. If you don't, people won't be able to find you. However, you need to experiment to discover what fits and where you need to focus. Early in your business, be willing to try things that fit with your talents and allow time to clarify your focus. As you try things, find mentors and coaches to support you. The money you spend to support your work will come back to you.

Being BOLD serves you well

You must ask for what you need or you won't get it. Asking questions is a wonderful way to learn, grow, and find business opportunities. You will be remembered more for the questions you ask than the answers you give. If you see a speaker or a business person you admire, reach out. There might be a connection to be made, but it won't happen if you don't take the initiative and introduce yourself.

UXL

Margaret targets people who feel stuck in their current position or who are struggling to obtain the position that matches their capabilities and passion. UXL is geared toward people in a transition—whether experiencing a new boss, new promotion, new project, or new team—and need some guidance to make this a career-accelerating opportunity. Margaret works with individuals and teams that need support or the nudge to make a great impression, get the work done well, and leave the impact that reflects their capabilities.

www.youexcelnow.com

Angie Weber

Hello Life

"The entrepreneur bug bit and it bit hard!"

Angie Weber, co-founder of Hello Life, is on a mission to help women feel confident and embrace their beauty. As a mama of twins, she understands how crazy life can get. She is passionate about bringing easy-to-use and natural options to women to boost their confidence, whether putting on a little foundation or getting ready for a night on the town.

Angie co-runs a marketing company. An entrepreneur herself, she targets other entrepreneurs as clients. One day, she was meeting with a client and suddenly knew she was ready to become her own entrepreneur. Her intuition told her she was prepared and could tolerate the risks involved. Her first idea was a coffee shop. After further research and consideration of other options, she decided on cosmetics.

Angie's Advice ...

Have a bigger "why" behind your business

Angie's bigger "why" is to support mental health issues, including donating financially to organizations with a mission of mental health support. Without the "why," it can be tough to get through the challenges. Angie's "why" helps her set aside the challenge and keep moving forward with her passion and mission.

Delegate

As an entrepreneur, it is difficult to delegate. The money may not support your ability to hand over tasks. Or, your own perfectionism may not support your comfort in delegating. Angie found that if she learned the process of her business needs, she was more willing to delegate.

There are many pieces of entrepreneurship she did not enjoy—what a revelation when she realized there are people out there who love doing what she does not! Asking herself, "What is my time and stress worth?" made it easier to delegate.

Keep your money straight

Many entrepreneurs don't pay themselves first. That's a big mistake! This keeps your motivation low. Set up your accounting system to ensure you are managing your money effectively.

Have your support systems in place

Being an entrepreneur is as exhilarating as riding a roller coaster. Sometimes, things are going up and you get excited. Sometimes, things are going down and you think you might throw up! Have entrepreneur accountability partners to help you move through the tough days and celebrate the good ones.

Hello Life

Hello Life is a natural cosmetic line focusing on bringing out the beauty and confidence in a woman. They are also on a mission to make an impact in the world of mental healthcare by donating one dollar of each product purchased to awareness and research.

hellogorgeouslife.com

Rev. Dr. Rachel Wetzsteon

Rachel Wetzsteon, PhD

"It was stepping into my power."

Reverend Dr. Rachel Wetzsteon is passionate about healing, spirituality, and fully living in love. After years of studying health and teaching group fitness classes, she became attuned to other wellness factors that are often overlooked. These factors include mental, emotional, and spiritual connections. She came to her business when she began asking herself, "Why am I not feeling joyful?" She began asking questions and looking for something else. The process involved shifting many of her own beliefs about money and risk, as well as simplifying her life to focus on family. She allowed answers to come her way, leading to a new focus and direction from which her business eventually emerged.

Rachel's Advice ...

There might be a breakdown before a breakthrough

Sometimes, we need to become uncomfortable to move to a place of comfort. Even though certain times can seem devastating, new things will show up to move you in a new direction. Patience with yourself is important as you build and grow your business. In the midst of negative emotions, we need to keep moving forward and not allow those emotions to stop our movement. By doing this, we can allow the seemingly negative breakdown to guide us to new possibilities or even new breakthroughs.

This, or something better!

You need to have a vision, but be open to something better. There is probably more you can do than you think you can. Always ask for "this or something better." Guidance will arrive.

It isn't up to me – surrender!

There is a greater guide to assist you in your business. Operating your life and business from where you "should" or "have to" be will only bring you stress and block your business. When you hear yourself saying "should" or "have to," change the terminology to "get to." Let go of control and allow the process to emerge. Being present for what you need to do today brings inspired action.

Rachel Wetzsteon, PhD

Rachel is a teacher of spiritual growth and helps people shift into unconditional love, happiness, and healing. She is the author of *Radiantly Free*, hosts a podcast called *REV with Rachel*, and offers the app, *Rachel*, for download.

www.drrachelw.com

An Invitation From Cheryl

It is my hope to continue to support you and your business. There are several ways I can do so. I invite you to check out the following three options and see what fits for you and your business.

Be a listener

Join Cheryl on the *Straight Talk for Smart Business Women* podcast to hear more stories providing tips, tools, and ideas to support women-owned small businesses. You can find the podcast on iTunes, Google Play, Spotify, and Stritcher.

Be a guest on the show

If you would like to be a guest on the *Straight Talk for Smart Business Women* podcast, send an email to Cheryl@TheLeadershipEnergy.com. You will receive the guest interview packet to see if this opportunity fits for you and your business.

Let me continue to support you and your business growth

Straight Talk Business Conversations with Cheryl and the *Straight Talk for Smart Business Women Academy* are just two of the resources you will find on my website:

www.CherylLeitschuh.com

If you have ideas, questions, or suggestions on tools you need to support your business, please email: Cheryl@TheLeadershipEnergy.com.